Visible Analyst®

Tutorial on
Structured Methods
and the
Repository

D1401040

Printed and bound in the United States of America.

This manual was prepared using Microsoft Word for Windows 97.

Visible Analyst
Tutorial on Structured Methods and the Repository

Visible Analyst is a registered trademark of Visible Systems Corporation.

Microsoft and Windows are registered trademarks of Microsoft Corporation.
Other product and company names are either trademarks or registered trademarks of their respective owners.

Visible Systems Corporation
201 Spring Street
Lexington, MA 02421
Technical Support: 781-778-0200
Fax: 781-778-0208
Internet: http://www.visible.com
E-mail: support@visible.com

Table of Contents

Lesson 1

Getting to Know Visible Analyst

INTRODUCTION

CASE tools provide a foundation for defining, designing, building, testing, documenting and supporting information systems and software products. CASE tools are based on logical dissection of the real world into understandable models, processes and components. CASE tools provide mechanisms for evaluating current information activities, defining proposed changes, producing and validating new information processes and focusing on changes that will enhance the performance and operation of the organization. The successful use of CASE tools requires an understanding of the underlying concepts and logic and a comfortable knowledge of the operation and use of the CASE tool.

Visible Analyst has been created to make the implementation of CASE techniques a logical, flexible, natural and easy-to-perform process. Visible Analyst is a seamless CASE tool that integrates all phases of planning, analysis, design, code generation, and reverse engineering. Visible Analyst provides facilities for the development of function, object/class, state transition, data, data flow (process), activity, use case, sequence, collaboration, and structure chart (product) models for an information system. An integrated repository containing all defined model elements, extensive additional component definitions and free-form notes and definition fields provides a continuous life-cycle library of the design and development process. The Visible Analyst repository is used for reports of project content and to generate various forms of schema and application software code.

These lessons have been designed to lead you through the Visible Analyst mechanics and to demonstrate how easy Visible Analyst is to use. These lessons cover the entire development process, from drawing functional diagrams to generating program code. You can follow the lessons in sequence or you can select just the ones of interest to you. Like Visible Analyst itself, you have the flexibility to use any piece of the tool in any order that is reasonable within the project.

The tutorial also provides you with some insight into CASE concepts and underlying logic. These concepts are basically simple and logical. They allow you to break the complex real world into smaller and more manageable chunks that can be defined quickly and then be used to build operational pieces that *work* in the complex real world. Each of the CASE models provides a different view of the real world. Visible Analyst ties these models together and provides a vehicle for using them to define and evaluate current information operations. Proposed changes in the information processes, procedures and sequences are reflected into the CASE models and then are used to build a new set for the proposed change operations. The analysts, designers, developers and users interact with the Visible Analyst models and data repository to verify and validate the information steps and procedures for their organization and operations.

Once the architecture of the new information system is considered sound and solid, the software designer moves to defining and building the new product components and the software code. Visible Analyst supports the development of physical programming modules through the structure chart model. It also supports the definition and recording of pseudo code in the Visible Analyst repository. From these definitions and the data model, Visible Analyst generates database schema, SQL code and application shell code. Test plans, sequences, test cases and scenarios can also be generated in the repository notes fields.

FAST TRACK USERS

Those who like to work on the Fast Track should read Lesson 2 - Diagramming Basics and follow the steps for creating a project, creating a diagram, and some optional settings that are available with Visible Analyst. Lesson 2 gives you the basic skills for working with Visible Analyst. We recommend that you work through the other lessons to discover the more advanced features that make Visible Analyst a powerful tool. Throughout the tutorial are references to features that are not demonstrated in the tutorial but that may be of interest to you. You can find more information about these features in the *Operation Manual*. The online help feature in Visible Analyst, accessed from the **Help** menu or by pressing F1, also provides you with more information on the referenced subjects.

Note
☐ Since Visible Analyst is available in multiple configurations, the software you purchased may not include all of the diagram types or advanced features described in these lessons. The basic drawing techniques apply to all diagram types, and you are encouraged to work through the brief exercise in Lesson 2 - Diagramming Basics. Thereafter, you can skip chapters that do not apply to your Visible Analyst package.

OVERVIEW OF CASE CONCEPTS

CASE concepts involve creating and defining different models or views of the real world and then using these models to analyze and develop changes and modifications to the information processes of the organization. Some of the models provide definitions of factual items such as business functions, objects and data entities; others show how things flow, connect or relate to one another. Some of the models evolve and expand to match reality and others are done as snapshots, showing as-is and then as-proposed operations. The views are composed graphically using symbolic objects, line connectors and some rules of logic and structure. The objects are given names called labels, which populate the data repository with entries that can be retrieved, expanded, detailed and used to define and document the contents of the project. There are logic rules for many parts of the models. The models can be tested and evaluated for completeness, consistency, rule compliance and other factors. All of the models and the repository are interrelated; many share common components such as databases, objects and/or actions. The development of the models is iterative, often requiring several sessions before the models are complete and realistic. The ability to move from one model to another and to work on different ones at different times is critical to a successful CASE tool.

The rules of CASE deal with the checking of consistency and logical structures such as naming and complete linkages. Errors found in models are reported during the Visible Analyst *analyze* process. These errors should be corrected to maintain consistency and accuracy of the models. However, Visible Analyst, unlike software compilers, allows you to continue with any reasonable CASE operation without waiting until you have corrected all errors. This allows you to continue progress on the project and its components. However, it also leaves you responsible for returning and correcting your errors.

The Basic CASE Models

The basic CASE models include:

Functional Decomposition Model (also known as a Business Model) - Shows the business functions and the processes they support drawn in a hierarchical structure.

Entity Relationship Model (also known as a Data Model) - Shows the data entities of the application and the relationships between the entities. The entities are things and the relationships are actions. The data attributes can be defined for the entities via the repository and then shown on the diagram. Entities and relationships can be selected in subsets to produce views of the data model.

Object Model (also known as an Object Class Model) - Shows classes of objects, subclasses, aggregations and inheritance. Defines structures and packaging of data for an application.

State Transition Model (also known as the Real Time Model) - Shows how objects transition to and from various states or conditions and the events or triggers that cause them to change between the different states.

Process Model (also known as the Data Flow Diagram) - Shows how things occur in the organization via a sequence of processes, actions, stores, inputs and outputs. Processes are decomposed into more detail, producing a layered hierarchical structure.

Product Model (also known as a Structure Chart) - Shows a hierarchical, top-down design map of how the application will be programmed, built, integrated and tested.

Use Case Model – Shows the relationship between a user and a computer system.

Activity Model – Is a special form of state diagram where states represent the performance of actions or subactivities. Transitions are triggered by the completion of the actions or subactivities.

Sequence Model – Shows how objects collaborate in some behavior.

Collaboration Model – Shows an interaction organized around the objects in the interaction and their links to each other.

Repository or Library Model (also known as the Project Database) - Keeps the records of all recorded objects and relationships from the diagrams and allows for the definition of detailed specifics and extensions of the individual items. Used for evaluation, reporting and generation of details about the project and its products.

Visible Analyst Choices

Today systems designers have multiple choices. They can follow the Structured Analysis and Structured Design (SA/SD) approach and build on functions/processes, data models and product concepts; or they can follow the object-oriented approach and build class hierarchies, dynamic states and functional/process models. Both approaches can build better information systems and both cover similar aspects of information systems definition. However, both use different sequences of effort and focus on different aspects of the project. Visible Analyst allows you to choose either approach or to combine the approaches to develop a comprehensive product definition, design and development mechanism.

There are five keys to using Visible Analyst, or any CASE tool. The first key is to develop the discipline to apply and follow the steps and procedures of the technique. The second key is to develop skills in conceptualizing the CASE models to represent the real world requirements. The third key is to be consistent in how you define and describe the real world. The fourth key is to strive to be complete in the definition of all of the major parts of a real world application. The fifth key is to progress from the conceptual to the operational specifications and construction of a working information systems process.

VISIBLE ANALYST OVERVIEW

Visible Analyst is a Microsoft® Windows® application. Versions 7.1 and higher of Visible Analyst work with Windows 95, 98, 2000, 2003, XP and Windows NT. This section defines the overall structure of Visible Analyst and identifies some of its key operational characteristics.

Visible Analyst Architecture

The basic components of Visible Analyst are: a set of diagramming tools, a rules module, and a repository module. Diagramming tools are used to construct the "blueprints" of your target system. These lessons guide you in the creation of diagrams and provide you with basic information on the uses of the diagrams.

A system is designed and constructed according to rules, and the rules module manages the methodologies of Visible Analyst tools for you. Visible Analyst allows you to choose the rule set you prefer to use as a guideline for the development of your system. These rules are important in determining the appearance of your diagrams, as well as the entire structure of your system. For the purposes of the tutorial, you are introduced to the supported techniques and learn how to designate the rule set to use and the different symbol types used for each rules methodology.

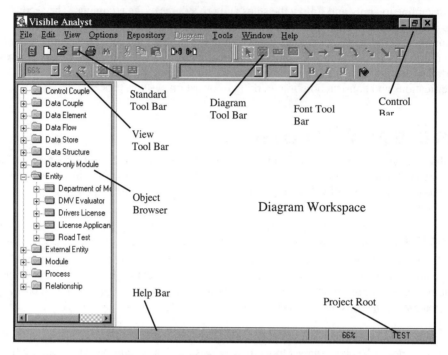

Figure 1-1 Visible Analyst Workspace

The repository module controls the individual repositories of each of your projects. A project repository stores detailed information about objects that are used in developing a system. An object in the repository includes processes, entities, relationship lines, classes, etc. The type of information contained in the repository for each object includes description, composition, values and meanings, location references, and other very specific detail information (see Lesson 14 - Repository Functions for details). The repository makes Visible Analyst a very powerful systems development tool. Visible Analyst is much more than just a diagramming tool; its repository and rules sets provide definition, documentation, and consistency capabilities for the entire system. Visible Analyst has advanced features enabling you to generate reports and code for your target system, using the information contained in a project repository.

Windows Version Features

This section highlights some of the Windows-specific features of Visible Analyst.

The Application Workspace

All work in Visible Analyst is done either in the main application workspace, shown in Figure 1-1, or in the repository, described in Lesson 14 - Repository Functions.

Windows Configuration

Visible Analyst configuration features controlled through Windows include the hardware configurations, desktop colors, available printer drivers, and available fonts. Changes or additions to these features can be made through Windows and are reflected in Visible Analyst.

Multiple Document Interface

The Windows Multiple Document Interface (MDI) allows multiple diagrams to be open at one time. Open diagrams can be of the same or different diagram types (data flow diagrams, entity relationship diagrams, etc.). Diagrams may be maximized, taking up the entire workspace, sized so that several diagram windows are visible, or minimized to icons appearing at the bottom of the application workspace. Any window larger than an icon is editable. You can cut, copy, and paste to and from the Windows Clipboard to move objects between diagrams and even between other Clipboard-aware applications. (See Figure 1-2.)

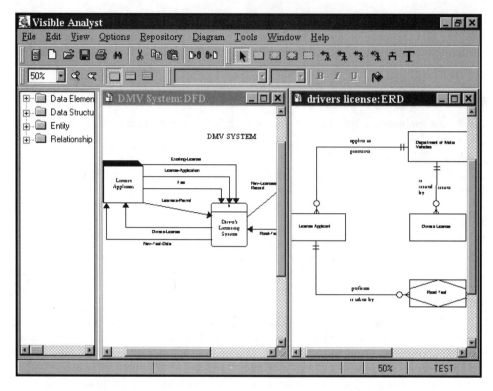

Figure 1-2 Visible Analyst Multiple Document Interface

Note

🗋 Users not familiar with MDI Windows programs should take note: there is a difference between the *diagram* Control menu button and the *Visible Analyst* Control menu button. The former is in the top left corner of the *diagram* window, or to the left of the File menu if the diagram is maximized. This Control menu contains functions that affect the diagram only, such as Maximize, Close, etc. The latter is in the top left corner of the *Visible Analyst* window. The *Visible Analyst* Control menu affects the whole Visible Analyst window and program.

Selecting a Diagram Object

A diagram object is anything that appears on a diagram: symbol, line, text, or block. When you click on an object with a mouse button, it becomes the *current* or *selected object* and you can perform various operations on it. There are five different ways to select an object. The following paragraphs describe the effect of selecting an object with the left mouse button, the right mouse button, a double-click with the left mouse button, and the TAB key; and selecting a group of objects as a block.

Left Mouse Button
Clicking on an object with the *left* mouse button selects it. The object changes color to show that it has been selected, allowing you to make changes to the object or to move the object. When a symbol or line is selected, text labels for that object are automatically highlighted.

Right Mouse Button
Clicking on an object with the *right* mouse button also selects it. In addition, the Object menu appears containing all of the functions that can be performed on that object.

Notes
☐ Unless stated to the contrary, instructions to *click* a mouse button refer to the *left* button. Instructions for the *right* button are explicitly mentioned.

☐ Left-handed mouse users: if you use a mouse with the buttons reversed, you should reverse references to left and right mouse buttons in this text.

Double-Click
If you double-click on an object with the *left* mouse button, the repository entry for that object appears. If the object is unlabeled, a dialog box for labeling the object is displayed. Double-clicking is also used to indicate the end of a line when drawing lines on a diagram.

TAB Key
To highlight only the text label for a selected symbol or line, press the TAB key until the appropriate item is highlighted. (If the label is located outside the symbol, you can click on it directly.) Continuing to press the TAB key sequentially selects each object on the diagram.

Selecting a Block
To select a block, meaning a group of objects on a diagram, click and hold the left mouse button and drag the mouse to draw a box around the objects. All objects *completely* contained within that box change colors to show that they are selected. Once a block is selected, you can perform various functions on the block such as cut, paste, move, change text settings for contained objects, and other actions.

Deselecting Objects
To deselect any object or block, simply click the *left* mouse button on an empty area anywhere on the diagram workspace outside of the object or block. The items that had been selected return to their usual color. You can also use the Clear function on the Edit menu.

Shortcut Keys

Shortcut keys provide fast access to functions without using the menus. Some of the active shortcut keys used in Visible Analyst are standard Windows shortcut control key sequences, such as CTRL+P, which is the command for Print; others are specific to Visible Analyst. All available shortcut keys are listed here.

CTRL+A	Analyze	Analyzes a diagram or entire project.
CTRL+C	Copy	Copies to clipboard.
CTRL+D	Define	Accesses the repository.
CTRL+E	Connect	Draws lines between selected symbols.
CTRL+F	Find	Accesses the search mode.
CTRL+L	Lines	Sets the cursor to line drawing mode.
CTRL+N	New Diagram	Creates a new diagram.
CTRL+O	Open Diagram	Opens an existing diagram.
CTRL+P	Print	Prints the current diagram or queue contents.
CTRL+Q	Report Query	Generates a custom repository report.
CTRL+R	Reports	Generates a standard repository report.
CTRL+S	Save	Saves the current diagram.
CTRL+T	Text	Sets the cursor to text adding mode.
CTRL+U	Clear	Deselects diagram object or block.
CTRL+V	Paste	Pastes from Clipboard.
CTRL+Y	Snap Symbols	Aligns selected symbols in a row.
CTRL+X	Cut	Cuts to Clipboard.
CTRL+Z	Undo	Erases partially drawn or undoes moved line.
DEL	Delete	Deletes object from diagram.
F1	Help	Displays context-sensitive help.
ALT+R	Repository Menu	Displays the Repository menu.
SHIFT+F1	Menu Help	Enters Help mode for menu items.
SHIFT+F10	Object Menu	Displays repository object menu.

Another standard Windows shortcut method for accessing a menu item without using the mouse is to press the ALT key followed by the underlined letter of the menu title or menu item that you would like to access. For example, to access the File menu, press the ALT key followed by the F key. It is not necessary to hold down the ALT key while pressing the F key.

Control Bar

The control bar, shown in Figure 1-3, is located above the diagram workspace and gives you quick access to commonly used functions and types of objects that can be added to a diagram. The control bar can contain up to four tool bars.

- The standard tool bar contains basic buttons, such as Select Project, Open Diagram, etc., common to most Windows applications.
- The diagram tools tool bar contains the symbol, line, and text buttons appropriate for the current diagram.

- The view tool bar contains controls that change the zoom level and entity/class view level.
- The font tool bar contains controls that allow changing the current font characteristics, such as font type, font size, etc.

You can customize the control bar by selecting Control Bar from the Options menu to display the Customize Control Bar dialog box. Using this dialog box, you can select the tool bars to be displayed and select control bar options such as Show Tooltips, Large Buttons, Flat Buttons, and Hot Buttons. You can also right-click the control bar itself to display a properties menu that allows you to toggle the individual tool bars on or off or to select the Customize option. To change the size and position of the tool bars, click the left mouse button on the "gripper" (the two vertical bars at the beginning of each tool bar) and drag the tool bar to the desired position. From the Customize Control Bar dialog box, you can also "undock" the diagram tools tool bar so that it appears in its own floating window.

The ⬉ button (shown in Figure 1-3) is used to change into selection mode (also called editing mode). In selection mode, objects can be selected on the diagram to be changed or moved, or a box can be drawn around many objects on a diagram, for moving, cutting and pasting, or changing text settings for groups of objects. Click one of the drawing mode buttons, and you can add that type of item to the diagram. The object types include symbols, lines, couples, and caption text. When you choose one of the drawing mode items from the control bar to add to your diagram, the cursor automatically changes to indicate that you are either in symbol, line or couple adding mode, or caption text adding mode. Specifically, this means that while the cursor is positioned inside the diagram workspace and it is something other than an arrow, which indicates selection mode, clicking on the mouse adds an object to the diagram.

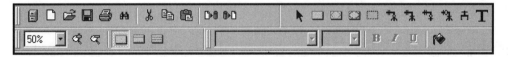

**Figure 1-3 The Control Bar for Entity Relationship Diagrams
with All Tool Bars Displayed**

For example, when the diagram tools tool bar is displayed on the control bar, you can easily select the particular symbol you want to add to the diagram. A symbol is added to your diagram centered at the cursor location anytime you click on the diagram workspace while the cursor indicates symbol drawing mode.

**Figure 1-4
The Symbol Cursor**

**Figure 1-5
The Line Cursor**

**Figure 1-6
The Text Cursor**

**Figure 1-7
The Couple Cursor**

Help Bar

As you move through the Visible Analyst menus, a line of text appears on the help bar at the bottom of the application workspace that briefly explains what that menu item does. The current zoom level, current project and current object are also displayed. You can toggle this feature off and on from the Options menu.

Object Browser

From the Options menu, you can choose to have the Visible Analyst object browser displayed on your screen. The object browser displays a list of all the objects in the repository in a resizable window. When there are no diagrams open, or the current window is the diagram list, all objects are displayed. When a diagram is open, only those objects that are valid for that diagram type are displayed. If an object appears on the open diagram, it is displayed in bold. Double-click on a folder in the list to expand or collapse it; double-click on an object in the list to display the Define dialog box. You can also click on an object in the list and drag it onto your diagram. To resize the object browser, click on the right margin of the browser and drag to the desired size.

Menus

The menus are arranged in nine groups for browsing and selecting the various features of Visible Analyst. (Refer to Figure 1-1.) Menu functions are more fully explained in the online help.

File Menu

The File menu contains the functions for accessing and creating projects and diagrams. This includes all of the functions that cause the opening of another diagram, such as Nest, Spawn, and Page. (These functions are explained under the specific diagram type where each is used.) It also includes a list of Recent Diagrams and Recent Projects. The Save, Print, and Exit functions are also found in the File menu. If you are using a network version, information about network activity and modifying the user list is contained in the File menu.

Edit Menu

The Edit menu contains the standard Windows editing functions including Cut, Copy, Paste, and Delete. There is also an Undo function for removing partially drawn lines and undoing a move line operation.

View Menu

The functions contained in the View menu allow you to change the appearance of the active diagram. There are functions to change the zoom level and to give you the ability to change the items displayed on a diagram, including Show Line Names, Show Symbol Names, Entity Display Options, Events, and Messages. Also on the View menu are Grid and Ruler, functions that make it easier to position objects accurately on a diagram.

Options Menu

The Options menu contains functions that allow you to change default settings for Visible Analyst. For diagram drawing and manipulation settings, the functions include automatic labeling of symbols and lines, Line Settings defaults, Text Settings defaults and diagram Colors, as well as on/off settings for Security, the Help Bar, the Object Browser, and the Control Bar. The Options menu also includes settings for model balancing rules, SQL schema and shell code generation, and user-defined attribute and object definition.

Repository Menu

All of the selections included in the Repository menu are functions performed on the information contained in a project's repository. These include Define, which allows repository access, schema and shell code generation, Key Analysis and Key Synchronization, Model Balancing, and repository Reports.

Diagram Menu

The Diagram menu contains functions for selecting, manipulating, and analyzing diagram objects. These include functions for selecting Symbols, Lines, or Text to add to a diagram, as well as functions for changing or stylizing a selected item on a diagram. The function for analyzing the diagrams according to the selected rules methodology, and the function for modifying an existing view are also contained in the Diagram menu.

Tools Menu

The Tools menu contains the various functions that can be performed on a project. These include Backup, Restore, Copy Project, Delete Project, Rename/Move, Import, Export, and copying information between projects. The utility for assigning user access to the multi-user version of Visible Analyst is also found in the Tools menu.

Window Menu

The Window menu allows you to change the arrangement of the open diagrams. Diagrams can be automatically arranged in a Tile, Cascade, or minimized (icon) format. You can also switch between open and minimized diagrams.

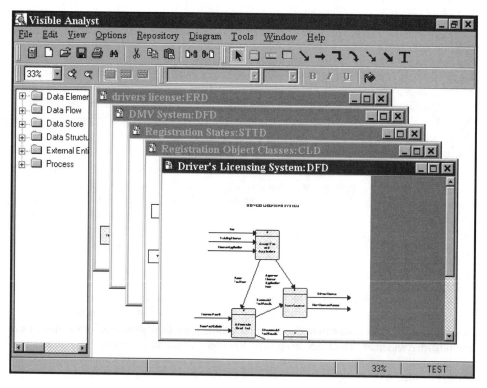

Figure 1-8 Cascaded Multiple Diagram Windows

Help Menu

The Help menu allows you to access the Help features, product and user information, and Visible Analyst on the Internet.

Lesson 2

Diagramming and Repository Basics

INTRODUCTION

This lesson introduces you to the diagramming tools. You learn the basic techniques for creating and modifying any type of diagram in Visible Analyst. We use the unstructured diagram format that does not require you to "follow the structured rules." This allows you to concentrate on the basics of the drawing process without worrying about rules and the repository. Sometimes you just want to draw a diagram, but not as a part of an analysis or design project. (A number of examples are shown the *Operation Manual*.) Also, some diagrams created from standard diagram types, such as cluster diagrams from entity relationship diagrams (ERDs) and process decomposition diagrams from data flow diagrams (DFDs), are always unstructured. You should know how to access them.

The basic techniques of drawing diagrams are valid for unstructured and structured diagrams. We could just as well use the DFD type or the ERD type to teach basic diagramming techniques, but not all users have a Visible Analyst version that contains all diagram types. However, all Visible Analyst packages have unstructured diagram capability. The diagram drawn in this lesson has no meaning other than as an exercise and is not part of any other lesson.

CREATING A NEW PROJECT

Each project that you create represents one complete system. One project could also be used to depict one unit in a very large system. By maintaining the entire system in one project, Visible Analyst ensures that the entire system remains consistent throughout the entire development process rather than checking for global consistency once all of the units have been merged together. The LAN version of Visible Analyst allows multiple designers to work on diagrams in the same project.

Note

☐ Different types of lines are available for each type of diagram. You can select the line type for any one of the other available diagram types for use with an unstructured diagram. This selection must be made before a diagram is created.

Open the Menu: 1   Click on the File menu with the *left* mouse button.

2   Select New Project. A dialog box like that in Figure 2-1 is displayed.

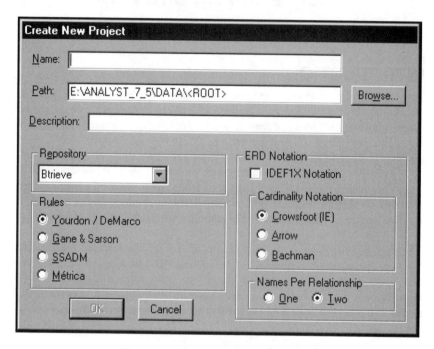

Figure 2-1 New Project Dialog Box

Name the Project: 3   Type TUTOR into the Project Name field. A project name or "root" can be up to 128 characters long. It must begin with a letter and can be composed of letters and numbers.

Describe the Project: 4   Click the cursor inside the field marked Description. Type "Tutorial Project." Another common method for moving the cursor to other fields in a dialog box is to use the TAB key. Try pressing the TAB key a number of times. The highlighted selection changes as the cursor moves to a new field. Press the TAB key until the cursor returns to the Description field.

The next steps help familiarize you with the options available when creating a project. If a default is incorrect, you can click on the item to change the setting.

Select the database Engine:	5	Choose Btrieve as the database engine. Btrieve is included with Visible Analyst.
Select the Rules to Apply:	6	In the box entitled Rules, select Gane & Sarson. This is where you choose the rule set you want applied to your project. An unstructured diagram does not follow any rules, but it is necessary to select the type of rules to be applied to all of the diagrams that might be created for this project. (Rules are covered in more detail in Lesson 6 – Data Flow Diagrams.)
Select ERD Notation Conventions:	7	In the area entitled ERD Notation, the default notation is Crowsfoot. This selects the type of relationship line notation you use on your Entity Relationship Diagrams. (This is covered in more detail in Lesson 5 – Entity Relationship Diagrams.)
	8	In the box entitled Names Per Relationship, the default is Two. This refers to how relationship lines on ERDs are labeled.
Activate the Project:	9	Click OK to activate the project. When you do this, the New Diagram dialog box is automatically displayed.

Now you have created a project. The name of your project is displayed in the lower right-hand corner of the application workspace. If you turned off the help bar from the **Options** menu, the project name is not displayed. The next step is to create a diagram.

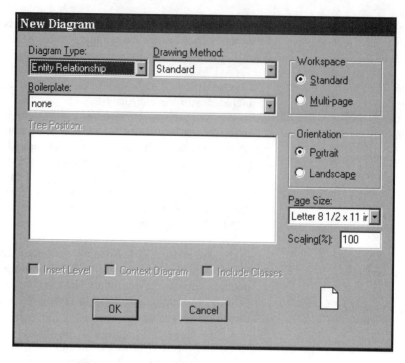

Figure 2-2 New Diagram Dialog Box

CREATING A NEW DIAGRAM

After creating a project and before creating a diagram, the screen should look just as it did when you started Visible Analyst, except that the name of your project appears in the lower right-hand corner. To create a new diagram, follow these steps:

Open the Menu:
1   Click on the File menu (or click the New Diagram button on the standard tool bar).

2   Select New Diagram. A dialog box like the one in Figure 2-2 is displayed.

Set the Diagram Type:
3   Open the selection box for the Diagram Type by clicking the arrow at the end of that field. Select Unstructured. The field marked Boilerplate should say None. A boilerplate is a template you can create to keep information such as diagram creation date, diagram created by information, and a diagram heading without rewriting it each time you

---

18

create a new diagram. (See the *Operation Manual* or the online help system for more information on boilerplates. Boilerplates are not enabled in the Education Editions of Visible Analyst.)

Select a Workspace: 4   In the area entitled Workspace, select Standard. This sets your diagram size to one page. Multi-page allows you to spread large diagrams over a workspace of 90 x 88 inches. You can go to larger pages as needed later, or select them now if you know you are going to work on a large diagram. (Multi-page is not enabled in the Education Editions of Visible Analyst.)

Select Orientation: 5   In the Orientation area, select Landscape.

Select Page Size: 6   Open the Page Size drop-down list and select 8-1/2 x 11.

Select Scaling: 7   Accept the default scaling, 100%.

Create the Diagram: 8   Click OK to open a blank diagram.

The control bar is located just above the diagram and below the menu. The ↖ button is highlighted.

Above the menus, notice the title of your diagram. Since it has not been saved, it is marked Untitled: US. The US indicates that the window contains an unstructured diagram.

EDITING A DIAGRAM

Adding Symbols to a Diagram

Now add symbols to the diagram to become familiar with the different methods for doing this.

Turn on Auto Label Symbols: 1   Open the **Options** menu. There should be a check mark next to the selection **Auto Label Symbols**. This indicates that you are automatically prompted to label a symbol as soon as it is drawn. If there is no check mark next to the selection, set the option by clicking on the selection.

Change to Symbol-Adding Mode: 2   Click the first symbol button in the control bar, then slowly move the cursor from button to button. As you move the mouse over each button, a brief description appears on the control bar describing its function. Icon buttons are added to the control bar for each type of symbol available to you for the current diagram type. Only certain symbols are available for most types of diagrams, but they are all available for an unstructured diagram. When you move the cursor back over the drawing area, it changes to indicate that you are in symbol adding mode

Position the Symbol: 3   Place the cursor where you would like the symbol to appear on the diagram and click the *left* mouse button. The symbol is drawn. Because **Auto Label Symbols** is turned on, a dialog box appears for labeling the symbol.

Label the Symbol: 4   Type "First" into the Text field.

    5   Click the OK button.

Repeat for Another Symbol: 6   Click the third symbol button and add it to the diagram as above.

    7   Type "Second" into the Text field and click OK. Note that the new symbol is now highlighted, indicating that it is the *current object*, and the previous symbol you added has returned to normal display.

Save and Label the Diagram: 8   From the **File** menu, select **Save**.

    9   Type the diagram label "Diagramming Technique."

    10   Click OK. The diagram label appears in the window title bar. (See Figure 2-3.)

Note

The only difference between saving a new diagram and saving an existing one is that you have to give the new diagram a name in the dialog box that is displayed. The only restrictions on diagram labels are that they cannot exceed 40 characters and that they must be unique within the diagram type of the project. To change a diagram's name select Save With New Name from the File menu. After that, the process is identical to that described for a new diagram, above.

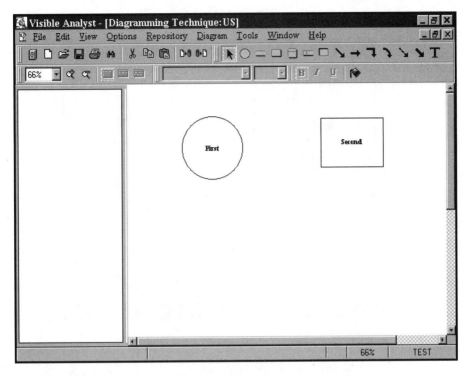

Figure 2-3 New Diagram with Symbols Added

Stylizing a Symbol

Change into Selection Mode:	1	Click the ↖ button on the control bar or press the ESC key. This changes the cursor, indicating that Visible Analyst is now in selection mode.
Use the Object Menu:	2	Position the cursor over the symbol labeled First and click on it with the *right* mouse button. A menu appears with functions that can be performed on the symbol.
	3	Select Stylize.
Stylize the Symbol:	4	In the dialog box, adjust the level of boldness by double-clicking the right-hand arrow on the scroll bar under the word Boldness.
	5	Click the Apply button. The symbol in the box indicates how your symbol looks. (See Figure 2-4.)

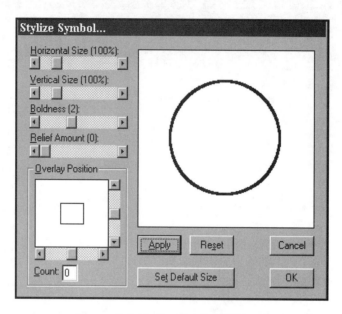

Figure 2-4 Stylize Symbol Dialog Box

6   Click the OK button and the stylization you selected is
           applied to the symbol on the diagram.

Moving, Cutting, and Pasting a Symbol

Select the Symbol: 1   Position the cursor inside the symbol Second and click the
                               left mouse button. The symbol changes color to show that
                               it is now the selected or current object.

Move the Symbol: 2   Position the cursor inside the symbol Second and click
                               and hold the *left* mouse button. Move the symbol by
                               dragging the box around. A rectangular outline, called the
                               "bounding box," appears in place of the symbol. Release
                               the mouse button when your symbol is where you want it
                               or press the ESC key if you want to cancel the move
                               operation.

Cut and Paste the   3   While the symbol is selected, click on the Edit menu.
Symbol:

                         4   Select Cut. The symbol disappears from the diagram,
                               but is saved on the Windows Clipboard.

5   Go back to the Edit menu and select Paste. The symbol is displayed surrounded by a dashed outline, indicating the symbol is the current object. Position the cursor within the outline of the symbol, hold the *left* mouse button down and drag it to the desired location on the diagram. Release the mouse button.

Deselect the Symbol: 6   Click on an empty space on the diagram with the *left* mouse button. This deselects the highlighted current object.

Notes

☐   You can use the Windows keyboard shortcuts for the editing functions to speed up these operations and to edit in dialog boxes.

☐   When selecting or changing line types and line terminator choices, Visible Analyst performs differently depending on what state it was in when the modifications were entered. When no diagram is selected and the line types are changed, the default choices are modified. When a diagram is selected but no line is highlighted, the choices remain in effect for the diagram. If a line is selected, the change only impacts the selected line.

Adding Lines to a Diagram

Now add a line to connect the two symbols you have drawn.

Turn on Auto Label Lines: 1   Open the Options menu. There should be a check mark next to the selection Auto Label Lines. This indicates that you are automatically prompted to label a line as soon as it is drawn. If there is no check mark next to the selection, set the option by clicking on the selection.

Set Line-Drawing Mode: 2   Click the first line button in the diagram tools tool bar to put Visible Analyst in line-drawing mode. The cursor changes to indicate this.

Draw the Line: 3   Position the cursor on the edge of the symbol labeled First that is nearest to the symbol labeled Second.

4   Press and hold the *left* mouse button.

5   Drag the line to the edge of symbol Second. The way the line stretches between the cursor and the start-point is sometimes called "rubber-banding."

6   Release the mouse button to signal the end of the line. If you release the mouse button within the symbol, the line is connected automatically to the edge of the symbol. When the line is completed, it changes color and *handles* appear at the endpoints. (See Figure 2-5.) A dialog box appears for labeling the line.

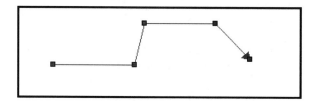

Figure 2-5 A Line With Its Handles

Label the Line: 7   Type "Flowname."

8   Click OK to draw the label next to the line on the diagram.

Now that you know how to add a line to a diagram, you can adjust the position and appearance of that line.

Note

▢   If you want to move the name of a line, select the name by positioning the cursor on the text and press and hold the *left* mouse button. Drag the label to the desired position and then release the mouse button.

Selecting and Adjusting Lines

Return to Selection   1   Click the ↖ button on the control bar or press the
Mode: ESC key.

Select the Line: 2   If the line is not currently highlighted, click on any point along the line. When a line is selected, you can see its *handles*, little boxes at the end of each segment that allow you to move the segments by dragging the handles with the mouse.

Set Line Characteristics:	3	From the Options menu select Line Settings.
	4	Choose Single Dashed for Line Type.
	5	Click OK. The line is redrawn using the new type.

Changing Line Settings as above allows you to adjust the line characteristics for the selected line. If no line is selected, you choose the characteristics for the next line you draw.

Adding Caption Text to a Diagram

You can add text in the form of a title or a paragraph. This text is used to enhance the definition of your diagram or its parts. When entering the text, press ENTER to continue the text on another line.

Set Caption Text Mode:	1	Click on the large T (text) button on the control bar.
Select the Caption Position:	2	Position your cursor at the top of the diagram and click with the *left* mouse button.
Enter the Text:	3	Type "Unstructured Diagram #1." Then press ENTER to move the cursor down to the next line. Type "Diagram Drawing Techniques."
	4	Click OK.
	5	Click the ↖ button on the control bar or press the ESC key to return to editing mode.
Change the Caption Characteristics:	6	Click the right mouse button over the caption you just added to display the Object menu for the caption.
	7	Select Text Settings from the Object menu.
	8	Select Times New Roman in the box labeled Typeface. Refer to Figure 2-6.

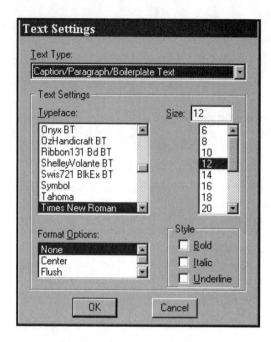

Figure 2-6 Text Settings Dialog Box

9   Change the Point Size to 16 in the Size box.

10   Select Bold in the box labeled Style.

11   Select Center in the box labeled Format Options.

12   Click the OK button and then deselect the text. The completed diagram should appear more or less like that shown in Figure 2-7.

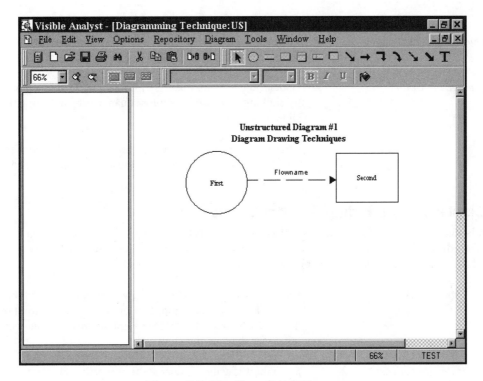

Figure 2-7 The Completed Diagram

Note

⬚ The "T" icon text should not be used to define symbols or lines. Only symbol labels are entered into the repository for rules based components. To label an unlabeled diagram object, click the object with the *right* mouse button and choose Change Item from the object menu.

OTHER DIAGRAMMING FUNCTIONS

Now we take a look at some of the other functions available to help you create Visible Analyst diagrams.

Colors

Different screen objects displayed in different colors makes it easier to distinguish them on the screen. You have a number of choices available that you can experiment with to find a pleasing combination.

Open the Menu:	1	To change the colors of your symbols, lines, and text select Colors from the Options menu.
Change the Color:	2	Under Object Type, select Symbol Color. Select a color by clicking on one of the color squares or by adjusting the slide bars.
	3	Click OK. If no objects are selected, the default colors are set. If objects are selected, only those items are changed.

Displaying and Hiding Symbol Labels

It is sometimes easier to see the overall layout of objects on a diagram if there are no text labels distracting your attention from the structure the diagram represents. Visible Analyst allows you to hide the labels of symbols and lines if you wish to do so.

Hide the Labels:	1	From the View menu, click Show Symbol Names. The symbol labels should disappear. (A check mark in front of this selection indicates that the symbol names are shown; otherwise they are not shown.)
Redisplay the Labels:	2	From the View menu, select Show Symbol Names again to reset the names to show.

Note

⬚ Turning line or symbol labels off is *not* the same as not labeling them. A line or symbol that has never been labeled *does not exist* as far as the repository is concerned.

Changing Text Characteristics for a Block of Diagram Objects

Select a Group of Objects:	1	Draw a box around the symbols on the diagram. Place the cursor in the upper left corner of the diagram and hold the *left* mouse button down while you drag the mouse to the lower right corner of the diagram. A bounding box rectangle is created as you drag the mouse. After you release the button, all items *completely* inside the bounding box are highlighted.
Change the Text:	2	From the Options menu, select Text Settings.

3   Choose Symbol Labels in the box marked Text Type.

4   Choose a Typeface and Point Size.

5   Return to the Text Type box and choose Line Labels.

6   Choose a Typeface and Point Size.

7   Click OK.

8   Click in an empty area outside of the bounding box to deselect it.

The symbol labels and line labels for the items *completely* contained in the box change to the new text settings.

Note

◻   The text values of *all* items in the bounding box are set by this function. Those text types that you do not *explicitly* set revert to the default values shown in the dialog box.

CLOSING A DIAGRAM

To close a diagram:

Activate the Control Menu: 1   Click on the *diagram* Control menu button (not the *Analyst* Control menu button) in the top left corner of the *diagram* window, or to the left of the File menu when the diagram is maximized. There is also a Close Diagram function on the File menu.

    2   Select Close. If your diagram has not been maximized, meaning that it occupies less than the entire Visible Analyst workspace, you can close the diagram by double-clicking on the Control menu button.

    3   Visible Analyst prompts you to Save the diagram. Click Yes to close the diagram. Selecting No closes the diagram without saving any changes made since the last Save operation was performed.

THE TUTORIAL PROJECT

For the rest of this tutorial, you add diagrams to an existing project. We created the project to save you the time it would take to enter the repository information and create the diagrams that are necessary to demonstrate some of the more advanced features of Visible Analyst. To access the TEST project:

1   Choose Select Project from the File menu, or click the File Cabinet button on the control bar.

2   Select TEST from the list displayed on the Select Project dialog box and click OK.

TEST is now the current project. As when you created the first project, the lower right corner of the Visible Analyst screen displays the name of the current project.

CONCLUSION

Now that you understand the basic methods for drawing symbols, lines, and text in Visible Analyst, as well as how to change some of the optional settings, you are ready to build more significant diagrams.

We have provided diagrams to help demonstrate some of the structured modeling capabilities of Visible Analyst. The objects on the diagrams and entries in the repository have been filled in for you.

Lesson 3

Structured Modeling Techniques

OVERVIEW

The techniques for planning, process modeling, data modeling, object modeling, state transition modeling and structured design assist in the creation of systematically correct and consistent diagrams and documentation. Using structured and object techniques forces a standardization of logic throughout the system under analysis. The benefits of this approach are obvious:

- Large systems can be partitioned into component subsystems or subfunctions for further analysis.
- Specifications for individual components are easier, faster, and more accurate to define than the total system.
- The interaction between the parts can be planned, designed, evaluated, and implemented to reflect improved information flows and controls.
- More than one person can work with the same system in the network edition.
- Standardized format and grammar enhance and simplify communication and maintenance.

STRUCTURED PLANNING

Planning uses a structured technique based on functional decomposition for describing interrelationships among broad organizational areas, specific organization functions, and the systems that support those functions. Structured planning establishes organization responsibilities at function levels and then defines the process responsibilities within functions.

The objective of structured planning is threefold:

- To identify the specific business or organization function, including roles, goals, and objectives, to be automated or reengineered.
- To identify the existing system processes that support that function.
- To provide a focus for requirements analysis in support of identified goals and objectives.

For example, functions or functional areas in an organization that could be decomposed could be Finance, Sales, and Research. A function is usually designated by a *noun*. These functional areas could then be subdivided into processes that are groups of activities necessary in running the organization. The processes are usually defined in active state *verbs*. For example, the Sales function could be decomposed into the Customer Relations, Selling, and Management processes. These processes could then be further decomposed using a data flow diagram. If a process is labeled as a noun, it is a signal that the process should be further decomposed into more processes.

Because of the high-level functional nature of this type of modeling, the technique specifically applies to functions and not to the data that those functions use. Since functional decomposition modeling is viewed as the highest level of business planning, it is probably the place to begin when you wish to define the overall functioning of an enterprise. There is no rule that you must begin here, but other things are easier if you do. For designing individual projects, it may be just as effective to start with a process model or a data model (or both at once), for you might consider that the project does not have the breadth to warrant planning at the FDD level[1]. You might also choose to focus on the definition of objects, beginning with the object/class model.

ENTITY RELATIONSHIP MODELING

When designing, developing, restructuring, or maintaining a system, it is important to be able to model the interrelations of the data used in it. The technique used by Visible Analyst for representing data is known as entity relationship modeling or data modeling. The purpose of this technique is to graphically demonstrate how entities are related to one another. An entity represents a real or abstract thing that is important to an enterprise about which data needs to be stored. For example, an entity could be Customer, Product, Inventory, Supplier, Sale, Purchase Order, or some other label generally in the form of a singular noun. An entity would typically correspond to a table in a relational database.

The diagramming technique used to graphically depict the data model is the entity relationship diagram (ERD). It provides a clear and concise method for describing data through the use of entity symbols that are interconnected by relationship lines. Relationships between entities consist of specific associations that are described in terms of their *cardinality* and are generally labeled using action verbs. Cardinality refers to the numerical scope of associations between entities, such as a one-to-one association (one sale is associated with one customer); a one-to-many association (one supplier supplies many products); or a many-to-many association (many salesmen sell many products). The terms "one-to-one," "one-to-many," and "many-to-many" are common statements used to describe the cardinality of a relationship. There are specific ERD symbols used to signify cardinality, the terminators on relationship lines.

---

[1] Some of the theory behind functional decomposition diagrams can be found in Martin, J. and McClure, C., *Structured Techniques for Computing,* Prentice-Hall, Englewood Cliffs, NJ, 1985.

Relationships are also allowed to be optional instead of mandatory. It is sometimes the case that two entities are related, but not in all instances. For example, an employee can be assigned to zero, one, or many projects. The optional relationship is important when specifying a system in which the software is to enforce referential integrity; that is, to make sure that nothing is inserted into or deleted from the database that would make nonsense of some other entry. For instance, one sale is associated with one or many sale items, but it would be wrong to have one without the other. The optional relationship enforces clear designation of what information can be omitted from or is optional within the database without disrupting other references.

A relationship is intrinsically bi-directional and can be thought of as consisting of a relationship in one direction and a reverse relationship in the other. Generally, each direction in a relationship is given its own name or label. If you think of a relationship in one direction as a sentence, subject–verb–object, entity1–relationship–entity2, the picture becomes very clear.

Some feel that entity relationship modeling should be the starting point for designing a system because it is necessary to know the nature of the data in order to determine the processing done upon it. Others feel that the process model is the best starting place because the processing of the data *is* the system, and the data and its storage can be designed to fit the necessary processing. Visible Analyst accommodates either approach and allows you to build upon what you have done before. You can then use the diagrams you created and the repository information captured from them to refine the description of your model and to help you in properly normalizing[2] the data.[3]

PROCESS MODELING

Process modeling, otherwise known as structured analysis, is a technique for graphically depicting a system. The process modeling technique describes a system by focusing on the transformations of data inputs and outputs by processes. Whether examining an existing system or designing a new one (or both), this is a key step toward fully understanding the

---

[2] Normalization is a means of eliminating redundancy in data. It is a complex topic and is beyond the scope of this tutorial. Since understanding normalization is key to effective database design, you should consult a text on the subject, such as one of those written by C. J. Date.

[3] Although many of the methodological details are different from how it is done in Visible Analyst, a good introduction to the concepts of data modeling can be found in Shlaer, S. and Mellor, S. J., *Object-Oriented Systems Analysis*, Prentice-Hall, Englewood Cliffs, NJ, 1988.

A practical, but more advanced, book is Fleming, C. C. and von Halle, B., *Handbook of Relational Database Design*, Addison-Wesley, Reading, MA, 1989.

system. The diagrams you draw allow you to show, at levels of increasing detail, how data flows through your system and what is being done to it along the way.

Specifically, process modeling is used to identify the data flowing into a process, the business rules or logic used to transform the data, and the resulting output data flow. It demonstrates for a business area or a system where the data comes from, what processes transform it, and how processes interact with data stores.

The diagramming technique used for process modeling in structured analysis is the data flow diagram (DFD). The DFD consists of data flows, processes, data stores, and external entities. A data flow is data that is in motion in your system. It is represented by an arrow that indicates the direction of the flow of data. A data flow is labeled as a noun, indicating the particular data that is being transferred. A process is a procedural component, a transformation agent, in the system. It transforms inputs to outputs. A process is indicated by an action verb describing the sort of transformation that occurs. For example, Prepare Bank Deposits would designate a process. A data store, also called a file, represents a *logical* file, a database, or even a filing cabinet. In a system, it is data at rest within the scope of the system. An external entity, also called a source/sink, provides data to the system from outside the scope of the system, or receives data from the system. External entities are outside the system, so they are beyond the scope of analysis. A data store, a source, and a sink are all generally labeled as nouns.

A number of methodologies are available for process modeling. The most widely used are Yourdon/DeMarco, Gane & Sarson, SSADM, and Mètrica. Visible Analyst implements these techniques. There are few differences among the techniques. The most noticeable is the slightly different appearance of the symbols used. The symbols are also named somewhat differently. For a detailed description of the differences, please refer to the Visible Analyst *Operation Manual* or to the online help system[4].

The methodology you use is up to you. They are equally useful, and the results are the same. The data flow diagramming tutorial uses the Gane & Sarson methodology; but since they are so similar, it shows you the basics of how all are used.

---

[4] For more detailed information on these analysis methodologies, you can refer to the following books:

       DeMarco, Tom. *Structured Analysis and System Specification.* Englewood Cliffs: Prentice-Hall, 1978.

       Gane, C. and Sarson, T. *Structured Systems Analysis: Tools and Techniques.* Englewood Cliffs: Prentice-Hall, 1979.

WORKING WITH BOTH DATA AND PROCESS MODELS

All information you place in any diagram is, of course, captured by the repository and is available to both your process models (DFDs) and to your data models (ERDs) (where applicable) if you have an integrated tool set. The Analyze function can assist you in balancing a data model against a process model and in maintaining consistency.

There is some degree of correspondence between the entities in a data model and the data stores in a process model. The nature of this correspondence is not generally agreed upon. You may find that specifying such a correspondence helps you to insure that all data is accounted for between your models. You can specify that every entity must correspond to a data store with the same composition; Model Balancing notifies you if this is not the case.

Similarly, you can configure Visible Analyst to notify you of any data elements that have been defined but are not used. In other words, is there an element listed as part of an entity but not used by at least one process on at least one data flow diagram? Refer to the manual or the online help system for details about both balancing options.

Another link between your process and data models is the ability to create a view of that portion of your data model affected by a particular process. Once you have at least a portion of each model built, you can request that Visible Analyst draw a process view of your data model for a particular process. This shows you on a process-by-process basis how your data is used and how a designated process affects other data. This technique is demonstrated in Lesson 5 – Entity Relationship Diagrams.

STRUCTURED DESIGN

Structured design is the partitioning of a system into a hierarchy of modules that performs the activities internal to your system. It is a technique used for representing the internal structure of a program or system and its components. Structured design is a discipline that is complementary to structured analysis and implements another stage in the software life cycle. If data flow diagramming is the "what" of your system, structured design is the "how." To be most effective, it should be based upon specifications derived using structured analysis. The capability to integrate analysis and design verifies that your designs reflect the reality of your specifications.

The modeling technique used in structured design is the structure chart. It is a tree or hierarchical diagram that defines the overall architecture of a program or system by showing the program modules and their interrelationships. The structural information contained in the system model is used by Visible Analyst in the code generation process to create the precise infrastructure of your system. This includes the passing of control and parameters between program modules, as well as the specific order in which the modules are arranged in your code.

A module represents a collection of program statements with four basic attributes: input and output, function, mechanics, and internal data. It could also be referred to as a program, a procedure, a function, a subroutine, or any other similar concept. A structure chart shows the interrelationships of the modules in a system by arranging the modules in hierarchical levels and connecting the levels by invocation arrows designating flow of control. Data couples and control couples, designated by arrows, show the passing of data or control flags from one module to the next. This is equivalent to passing parameters between functions or procedures in an actual program.

The Visible rules implementation of the Yourdon/Constantine structured design methodology is intended to maintain as much design freedom as possible for you, while guarding against known poor design practices. The error and warning messages generated are intended to be used as guidelines rather than rules.[5]

OBJECT-ORIENTED MODELING

Object-oriented modeling concentrates on developing a collection of discrete objects that incorporate both data structure and behavior. The objects perform or are impacted by operations that represent the action between objects. The focus is on building object definitions that can be organized into a class hierarchy with high level abstractions of a class of like objects that provide inheritance of characteristics to subclasses and eventually to individual instances or a unique occurrence. Objects can be brought together into groups called aggregations, and they can have relationships and attributes (called properties) similar to those found in the entity relationship model. In fact, the data model (ERD) is the basis for object-oriented concepts with its entities and attributes.

OBJECT CONCEPTS

The object model is used to define and build the classes and subclasses of objects and the data characteristics that uniquely define object groups. By developing a clear picture of object structures and operations needed to support a business process, the designer can build reusable object components and save time and effort in the development and testing phases of

---

[5]For more detailed information on the Yourdon/Constantine structured design technique you can refer to the following books (the Page-Jones book is the better choice for beginners):

Page-Jones, M. *The Practical Guide to Structured Systems Design.* Englewood Cliffs: Prentice-Hall, 1988.

Yourdon, E.N. and Constantine, L.L. *Structured Design: Fundamentals of a Discipline of Computer Program and Systems Design.* Englewood Cliffs: Prentice-Hall, 1986.

the project. The object model is a static model in that it defines all of the objects that are found in the application and the general and specific characteristics of each object.

The object model shows a static snapshot of the hierarchy and packaging of the objects. The data model is a static snapshot of the data components of the application and the relationships between data components. The data flow diagram (process model) shows the flow and sequence of operations of the application. The state model shows the dynamic changes that occur within the applications and to the objects over time. The structure chart (physical model) defines how the application is assembled and built.

STATE TRANSITION (DYNAMIC) MODELING

The state transition model focuses on the changing conditions and states of an object. As an object such as a Customer Order progresses through an organization, it changes its state from a pending order to a shipped order to a paid order. The movement of the order from one state to another changes some of the object's properties and is usually caused by an event or a method being applied to the object.

The dynamic model is built after the object model is defined. It provides a sequence of states of the objects as they change over time. Thus the object model is static and complete, and the state (dynamic) model is continuously changing with different events and triggers. The state model is closest to reality and supports the programming design mechanics. If the programs cover all of the state transitions of the objects, then the system should fit to reality.

The object and the state-transition model are linked to the functional model that describes the data transformations of the system. The functional model can be represented by data flow diagrams with processes and data flows showing how objects are serviced through their time sequence transitions.[6]

OBJECT MODELING AND PROCESS MODELING

From the static snapshot of the objects, to the dynamic changes of states, to the sequence of operations in the data flow, to the build specifications of the structure chart, to the performance of activities, to the relationship between a user and a computer system, to how objects collaborate, object-oriented methodologies provide a complete mechanism for defining, designing and building information systems. Object concepts provide an alternative and a complement to the structured design methodologies. Both approaches define the data

---

[6]For a detailed discussion, refer to:

Rumbaugh, Blaha, Premerlani, Eddy and Lorensen. *Object-Oriented Modeling and Design*. Englewood Cliffs: Prentice-Hall, 1991.

components of the application and provide a view of how the application needs to act to provide service and support to the application users. The differences are mainly in the focus on components, the order of occurrence and the formats of packaging.

Both techniques and methodologies link to the happenings of the real world. They must both produce working information systems. They also share many similar concepts, such as reusability, modularity and hierarchical structures.

Visible Analyst supports both approaches to systems design and development. They can be used separately, together, or in any combination that suits you. Through the integrated Visible Analyst repository and the independence of the diagrams, you can maintain maximum flexibility and still take full advantage of the engineering practices for designing and developing better information systems.

DATA AND OBJECT RELATIONSHIPS

There is considerable similarity between entity and object models. Both focus on defining physical components: in the entity model the only elements are data or data-oriented components; in the object model, the focus is on real components that can be data, physical units, goods, materials, etc.

The general consideration is that the object model follows the design of the data model, but has made the application more worldly and generic.

LIBRARY MODEL

The library model contains the recorded information about all the pieces, parts, components, actions and conditions of the project. As objects are placed on diagrams and labeled, the label creates an entry in the library database for the proper data logic to support the type of graphic object. The library model is dynamic and evolutionary and is used to describe all the known factors and facets of the application and the systems development project. The Visible Analyst repository is the implementation of a comprehensive library model. It contains all of the labeled parts of the diagrams, and it provides a facility for expanding the details and definition of many components of the project. The Visible Analyst repository can support the building of data elements, database keys, pseudo code, test data and other specifications of the application. Free-form notes and description fields allow recording extensive comments, findings, important information, and other relevant factors about project components. Detailed reports and the generation of database schema, shell code, and other useful project outputs are derived from the library model.

The library model can serve the project design and development process, and it can be a useful reference source for maintenance and operation of the system as well as a key resource when changes need to be made to the system.

Lesson 4

Planning and Using Functional Decomposition Diagrams

OVERVIEW

In Visible Analyst, planning is done with functional decomposition diagrams (FDDs). They give you the ability to do high-level planning of business functions and their hierarchical relationships while concurrently populating the repository. You can enter business functions that you define onto diagrams and break them down into successively finer gradations. At some point, one that is entirely up to you, you can break down business functions (hereafter called simply functions) into processes. These processes are semantically equal to the processes that appear on data flow diagrams. The processes can themselves be broken down into smaller parts (still lower-level processes) on the FDDs.

The FDD is typically derived in close association with the user community. As they describe their organization responsibilities, it translates into functions. Once they begin describing "what" they do, it indicates the transfer to processes. This is the point at which you want to show finer gradations of functionality as processes. You can lay out all of the processes of this branch of your functional decomposition diagram, together with their hierarchical relationships. You can then instruct Visible Analyst to produce a set of DFDs for this branch of processes. This procedure is called "spawning" DFDs from an FDD function. You can then work on the DFDs and add data flows, files, external entities, etc. See Figure 4-1.

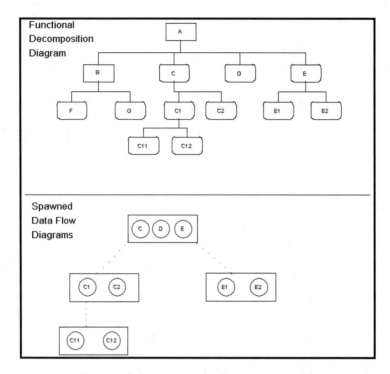

Figure 4-1 DFDs Created by an FDD Using Spawn

This lesson leads you through the process of creating a functional decomposition diagram. It also introduces you to a number of new techniques that you use frequently with Visible Analyst. The technique of spawning is also demonstrated.

As you create FDDs, repository entries are created. When you show hierarchical relationships between functions and/or processes, they are known to Visible Analyst, even though you cannot see them if you look in the repository. Since there is some overlap in repository support between DFDs and FDDs, it is significant which rules methodology you chose when you create a project. You can analyze your FDDs, either individually or as a group, to locate inconsistencies and violations of methodology rules. The types of analysis and the Analyze function are explained below.

Note

☐ A *functional* decomposition diagram is very different from a *process* decomposition diagram. The former is a full diagramming methodology for doing business planning. The latter, discussed in Lesson 6 – Data Flow Diagrams, is simply an unstructured diagram laying out the hierarchy of processes that are descendants of an indicated process.

DEFINITIONS

There are four meaningful things that appear on FDDs (see Figure 4-2):

Function	A function is denoted by a rectangle. It is the first of the three symbol buttons that appear on the control bar.
Process	A process is denoted by a rectangle with rounded corners. The conceptual dividing point between functions and processes is arbitrary and entirely up to you. The process symbol is the second symbol button on the control bar.
Connector	The lines between functions, between processes, and from functions to processes are called simply "connectors." They allow you to specify the hierarchical relationships between the functional elements of your model. The higher-order symbol can be referred to as a "parent" and each of the lower-order symbols connected can be called a "child" of the parent. The connectors between processes represent the same type of parent/child relationships as exist on DFD. Processes with the same parent would appear on the same DFD once the parent function has been "spawned." This technique is explained further in this lesson. There are three line buttons that appear on the control bar.
Page Connector	Unlike a data flow model, which occupies a tree-like structure of different diagrams at various levels of detail, a functional decomposition diagram is conceptually all one diagram. If a large model appeared entirely on a single page, it would be unreadable, so you are free to spread it over as many pages as you like. (Although not available in the Education Editions, you could also use a multi-page diagram.) Visible Analyst is able to keep the details straight if you indicate how the pages are linked by using page connectors. The page connector symbol is the third symbol button on the control bar and is identical in appearance to the off-page connector for structure charts.

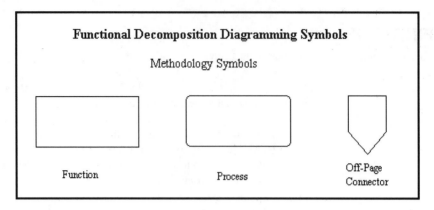

Figure 4-2 FDD Symbols

CREATING AN FDD

Adding Symbols to an FDD

Next you add symbols to create a very general functional decomposition diagram. The symbols are arranged in a hierarchical fashion, with the lower-level process symbols at the bottom. The description for adding symbols is brief because it is assumed that you have reviewed Lesson 2 – Diagramming Basics that covers adding symbols.

Create a New Diagram:	1	Create a new diagram by selecting New Diagram from the File menu or the new diagram button. Choose Decomposition and click OK.
Maximize the Diagram:	2	If you have other diagrams open, click the Maximize button in the top right corner of the window. Set the zoom level to 66% from the View menu or by clicking the right mouse button on the zoom level indicator at the bottom of the screen or use the zoom level buttons on the control bar.
Add Symbols:	3	Click on the first symbol button, the function symbol, and add four functions: Department of Motor Vehicles, Registration Department, Licensing Department, and Motor Vehicle Regulation Department. (Refer to Figure 4-3.)

It is not always easy to make your symbols line up in well-ordered rows. You can increase the zoom magnification so that you can see small details better. You can also turn on Grid, from the **View** menu, to give you a framework for positioning objects. If all you want to do is align symbols in horizontal or vertical rows, there is an easy alternative.

Align the Symbols:	4	Click the ↖ button on the control bar, the selection mode button.
	5	Select into a block the symbols you want to line up in one horizontal or vertical row by drawing a box around them with the mouse cursor. All symbols *completely* enclosed in the block are highlighted.
	6	Choose **Snap Symbols** from the **Diagram** menu. Your symbols are aligned.
	7	Click the mouse on some open area outside the block to deselect the symbols.
Add More Symbols:	8	After returning to symbol entry mode using the control bar, click on the process symbol (the second symbol) and add the three processes: Registration System, Driver's Licensing System, and Regulation System. Then align the processes. (Refer to Figure 4-3.)

Note

☐   If you need more room at the bottom of the screen to add symbols, you can use the window scroll bars or the PAGE DOWN key.

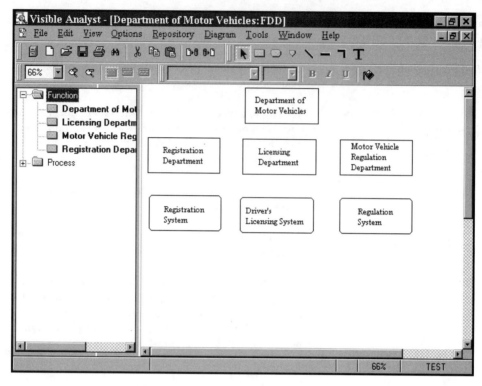

Figure 4-3 Function and Process Symbols Drawn on FDD

Now add lower-level processes to the current diagram so that you can practice spawning.

Add More Processes: 9   Below the process labeled Driver's Licensing System add a process labeled "Issue License." This is the name of a process contained in the second-level DFD provided with the TEST project.

Note

⬜ Since processes may exist in the repository, you can search for names during labeling by selecting the Search button on the Label menu. If the object browser is displayed, you can also click and drag an existing object from the browser onto the diagram.

10   Below Issue License add three processes: Get Photograph, Create License, and Update DMV Database.

Save the Diagram:	11	Select **Save** from the **File** menu. Name the diagram "Department of Motor Vehicles."

Adding Connection Lines to an FDD

Now add lines to establish the hierarchical relationships among the functions and processes on the diagrams. The line drawing process for a functional decomposition diagram is nearly automatic. Select into a block all of the symbols you want to connect and instruct Visible Analyst to connect them. You can also use a different method of selecting symbols into a block.

Enter Selection Mode:	1	Click the ↖ button on the control bar.
Make a Block:	2	While pressing the SHIFT key, click the *left* mouse button on the function labeled Department of Motor Vehicles. The symbol changes colors to show that it has been selected, and a box is drawn around it.
	3	While holding down the SHIFT key, click the function labeled Licensing Department. Repeat the procedure for Registration Department and Motor Vehicle Regulation Department. The selection box expands to encompass each new symbol that you select using SHIFT+click. If you select a symbol that you do not want in your line grouping, simply press the SHIFT key and click the symbol again to deselect it. See Figure 4-4.

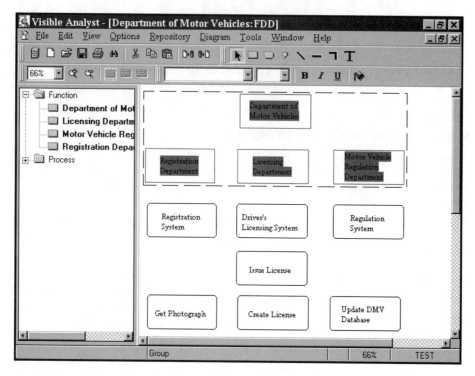

Figure 4-4 Connecting Selected Symbols

Connect the Symbols: 4 From the Diagram menu, select Connect. The connection lines are drawn automatically, as shown in Figure 4-5.

Note

☐ This function is designed to connect only two levels at a time; for example, a parent symbol and its children. If you select more levels into the block and connect, Visible Analyst assumes that there is one parent and that all of the other symbols are children of that parent.

5 Clear the block by clicking on an open area of the diagram outside the block.

Add More Lines: 6 Press and hold the SHIFT key and click the *left* mouse button on Licensing Department and Driver's Licensing System. The box expands to encompass these symbols.

7 From the Diagram menu select Connect.

8   Similarly, add connectors between Driver's Licensing System and Issue License and between Issue License and Get Photograph, Create License, and Update DMV Database.

9   Click on the first line button, and add a line between Registration Department and Registration System.

10   Click the first line button and add a line between Motor Vehicle Regulation Department and Regulation System.

11   Select the third line button, an elbow, and draw a connector between Driver's Licensing System and Motor Vehicle Regulation Department. (This is an error you are deliberately making that will be discovered by Analyze.)

Save: 12   Select Save from the File menu.

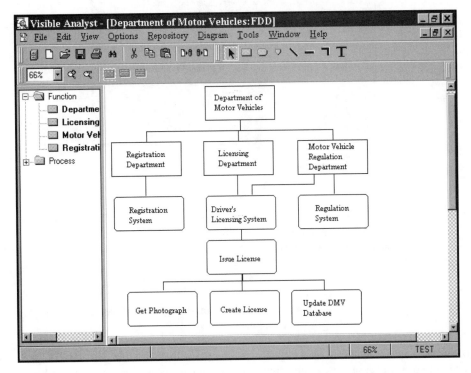

Figure 4-5 Functions with Connector Lines Drawn

Analyzing an FDD

Now use the Analyze function to check the diagram for correct syntax.

Analyze the Diagram: 1   Select Analyze from the Diagram menu. Be sure that Current Diagram and Syntax Check are selected. Click OK. After processing, a dialog box appears; you can maximize it to see it better. You see an error message about the extra connection line attached to Driver's Licensing System, as well as warnings about process symbols that are not on data flow diagrams. These messages serve as a reminder that you may want to decompose these processes in order to have a fully defined project.

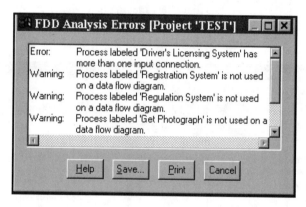

Figure 4-6 FDD Analysis Error Messages

Note

☐ You can keep analysis error dialog boxes on the screen while you carry on various Visible Analyst activities. This is to make it easier for you to correct the errors found by Analyze.

2   Click Cancel.

3   Click the ↖ button on the control bar, the selection mode button.

To make the diagram analyze correctly, you must remove the extra line you added to produce the above error. Because these connection lines are sometimes superimposed, it can be difficult to select the line you want; the wrong line may be selected when you click on an endpoint. However, a line can be selected by clicking *any* point on the line, not just at the endpoints. Since the line you drew has two right angles in it, it has two segments. At the junction of the segments there is a handle. Although the handle is invisible except when the line is selected, you can still click on it. (See Figure 4-7 where the positions of all of the line handles are revealed.)

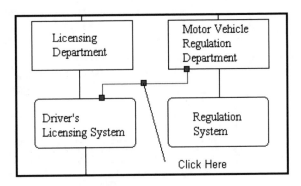

Figure 4-7 Select a Line by a Handle

Select the Line:	4	Click the *right* mouse button on any point of the line added between Driver's Licensing System and Motor Vehicle Regulation Department to display its **Object** menu. Make sure the line you have selected is the one you drew in step 11 of *Adding Connection Lines to an FDD*.
Delete the Line:	5	Select **Cut** or **Delete** from the **Object** menu to remove the line from the diagram. You can also delete the line by pressing the DELETE key or by selecting **Delete** or **Cut** from the **Edit** menu.

Note

☐ Visible Analyst asks you to confirm Delete but not Cut.

Analyze Again:	6	Run **Analyze** again. The diagram is correct, except for the warnings.

Note

☐ It is not necessary to save a diagram after **Analyze** has been performed because Visible Analyst automatically saves it for you before analysis begins. The **Save** option may not be available at various times. This means the diagram has already been saved.

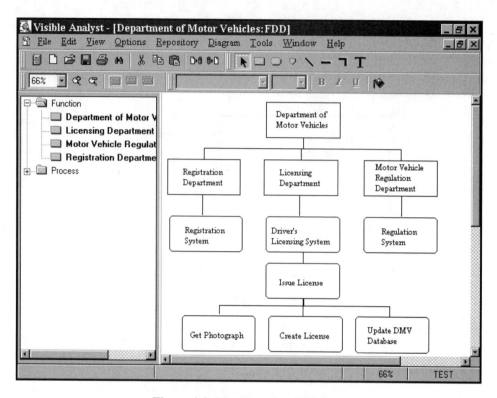

Figure 4-8 The Completed FDD

Generating DFDs from an FDD (Spawning)

The Spawn function is used to generate data flow diagrams from the decomposed processes contained on a functional decomposition diagram. The Spawn function only works with functions that have been directly decomposed into processes. This feature would not work for the function Department of Motor Vehicles or for any process on the diagram.

Select a Function:	1	Click the ✦ button on the control bar.
	2	With the *right* mouse button, click the function labeled Licensing Department.
Start Spawn:	3	Select Spawn from the Object menu and choose New DFD Set. This would ordinarily be used to create new DFDs, but a data flow diagram already exists containing the process Driver's Licensing System. There is also a

child diagram of that process containing the process Issue License. Therefore, Spawn checks for the existing connections and opens a dialog box explaining that it wants to add the three lower-level processes that you just created to a diagram that is given the name of the parent process of that diagram. In this case, it is Issue License.

Update Existing DFDs: 4   Click Update DFDs. Visible Analyst adds the three new processes to a DFD and opens the top-level DFD for you. This is one of the diagrams supplied with the TEST project and is displayed in Figure 4-9. You work with the spawned DFDs in Lesson 6 –Data Flow Diagrams.

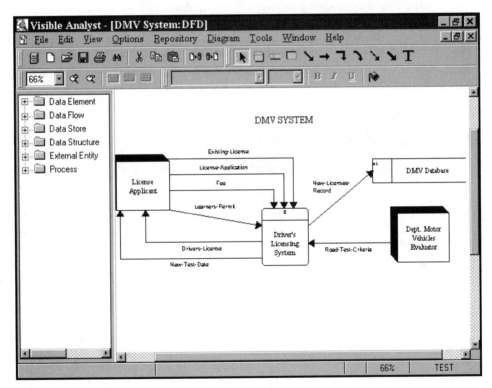

Figure 4-9 TEST Project Context Diagram

Notes

☐   If the error message "Decomposition hierarchy incompatible with data flows diagrams" is displayed, check the spelling of the process "Driver's Licensing

System." Make sure that the apostrophe s ('s) in the word "Driver's" is correct. To correct the spelling, click on the process "Driver's Licensing System" with the right mouse button and choose Change Item. Save the changes, and then perform the Spawn operation again.

☐ The spawn process produces detailed level DFDs. You must define, build, and then nest the appropriate higher level DFDs (such as the context diagram and the level 1 DFD) to the spawned ones. The spawn process can build a blank context diagram. You can add a context diagram, and then open and complete the spawn generated top level diagram. The Nest connectors still have to be built (see Lesson 6 - Data Flow Diagrams).

☐ The structured modeling technique (structured analysis and structured design) is used for the licensing application within the DMV, and the object modeling technique is used for the vehicle registration application. This illustrates the principles of each approach and also shows that Visible Analyst is flexible enough to allow either or both to be used within the same project.

What to do Next?

You now have a real life choice to make in pursuing the structured methodology life cycle. Having used the FDD **Spawn** function to build some intermediary DFDs, you can continue to build top-level DFDs and the overall data flow model. To do this, go to Lesson 6.

The alternative is to move to the data modeling process, build a data structure, and then return to the DFDs. To do this, continue with Lesson 5. The choice is entirely yours. You could also build part of your data model, then move to DFDs, and return later to finish or change your data model. Total flexibility with integration is a key feature of Visible Analyst.

Lesson 5

Entity Relationship Diagrams

OVERVIEW

This data modeling technique provides a precise method for detailing and illuminating the interrelationships of the data used by a system. You can depict the "entities" (see definition below) in the data you are modeling and the relationships between them by drawing them onto an entity relationship diagram (ERD). The data model (ERD) shows the major data objects of an application and how they fit together using the relationships. You can define the primary keys for the data entities and the composition of the data attributes of the entities in the Visible Analyst repository. (Defining primary keys and adding data attributes are explained in Lesson 14, Working with the Repository Functions.) The defined components can then be displayed on your ERD diagram by selecting these options from the View menu.

A diagram containing a picture of all or a subset of your data is called a "view." Each view can show an arbitrarily large or small part of your data model. You can show multiple views of your data model by including different combinations of entities and relationships on various diagrams. However, the entire data model, including the data elements composing each entity, is retained in the repository and can be accessed by creating a global view of the data model. This feature is explained in this lesson.

Definitions

The important diagram constructs in entity relationship data modeling include:

Entity
The entity (or, more properly, the entity type) is nothing more than a real-world object that you want to describe. The most generic type of entity is really a fundamental or independent entity, but is usually simply called an entity. It is composed of data elements (also called attributes), and you can describe these in the entity's repository composition field. A fundamental entity is an object or event. It is represented on an entity relationship diagram as a rectangle and is accessed by the first symbol button on the control bar.

Associative Entity   Another type is the associative entity (sometimes called a junction, intersection or concatenated entity, a gerund or a correlation table). This is basically a relationship (see below) about which you want to store information. It can only exist between two other entities. For example, the relationship between a customer and a product produces as a by-product the associative entity purchase order. A purchase order entity would not exist without the relationship between the other two entities. An associative entity is represented as a rectangle with straight diagonal lines across each corner. It is accessed by the second symbol button on the control bar.

Attributive Entity   The third entity type is the attributive or dependent entity. This is used to show data that is wholly dependent upon the existence of a fundamental entity. It is also used to show repeating subgroups of data. For example, the associative entity purchase order may have a dependent attributive entity named shipment showing the full or partial shipments that fulfill the purchase order. It is represented as a rectangle with rounded lines across each corner and is accessed by the last symbol button on the control bar.

Relationship   A relationship shows how one entity interacts with or can be affiliated with another entity. It appears on a diagram as a line drawn between two entities. Relationship lines ordinarily have two labels, one for each direction. The relationship lines can have terminators that show that the entities relate to each other on a one-to-one, one-to-many, or many-to-many basis (the relationship's cardinality), and whether the relationship is optional or mandatory. There are four line buttons on the control bar. Line types may be changed after they are drawn on the diagram.

Supertype/Subtypes   Specialized subtype entities can be created that are based on a generalized supertype entity and share common attributes. Only the attributes unique to the specialized entity need to be listed in the subtype entity. This is closely related to the object class inheritance concept. Visible Analyst also provides a detail field for specifying the exact number of relationships, if known. The supertype/subtype button is the fifth line button on the control bar.

Cluster   A cluster is a collection of entities and the relationships between them. It is not truly a part of your data model because it carries no new information. However, it can be very useful when you want to show very large data models on a single diagram and still have it comprehensible. You have the ability to cluster groups of entities and show these clusters and the relationships between them in summary fashion on a diagram. This limits the amount of detail on the diagram so that the larger outlines of what is contained in your data model are more visible. These objects are not available in the education edition of Visible Analyst.

A cluster is created in the repository and entities are added to its composition field. A cluster view can then be created by Visible Analyst to display the *pseudo*-relationships between clusters rather than real relationships between specific entities. The diagram Visible Analyst generates is an *unstructured* diagram, but the information contained in the diagram pertains to your entity relationship diagrams. For more information on Clusters, see the *Operation Manual* or the online help system.

View Object

A view object can be thought of as a derived or virtual table. It is composed of two components: a list of column names and a select statement used to filter information from the tables in the view. For each view; there is one primary select clause and any number of sub-select and union select clauses. Using the Define View dialog box, you select the tables and columns and define the join relationships, clauses and flags to be used by the view. For more information on view objects, see the *Operation Manual* or the online help. (View objects are not available in the Education Editions of Visible Analyst.)

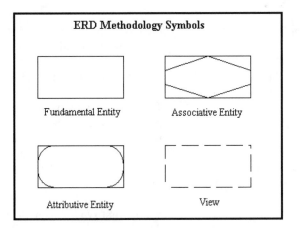

Figure 5-1 Entity Relationship Diagramming Symbols

Relationship Cardinality

Visible Analyst supports four different relationship cardinality notations: IDEF1X, Crowsfoot, Arrow, and Bachman. The type of notation you use is up to you, and you select it when a new project is created. The number of names per relationship line is also your choice. You can indicate one or two names per relationship. For this lesson, we use the standard Crowsfoot notation with two names per relationship.

If you select IDEF1X as the relationship cardinality when creating the project, the default notation is IDEF1X. You would then select Crowsfoot, Arrow or Bachman as an alternate cardinality notation.

DEVELOPING YOUR DATA MODEL

Each entity relationship diagram is complete in and of itself and shows one view of the data model of your project. (Remember that a view is a portion or subset of your entire data model represented on a single diagram. It should not be confused with a database view object.) When beginning your data model, you must manually add new entities and relationships to a diagram. After this has been done, you can create additional views by using the File menu View of Data Model function to select existing entities and relationships from the repository. Visible Analyst automatically draws the views for you. Then you can add to or subtract from each view and rearrange it as you wish. Thus you avoid having to draw portions of your data model repeatedly on different views.

Adding Entities to a View

Since the basic building block of the data model is the entity type (or simply, the entity) and since relationships cannot exist except to relate already existing entities, you begin by adding entities to a view.

Set the Zoom Level:	1	From the View menu, select 66% zoom so that you can see all of your needed workspace.
Create a New Diagram:	2	From the File menu, select New Diagram.
	3	Select the diagram type to be Entity Relationship with standard drawing method.
	4	Select the Page Size to be Standard.
	5	Click OK.
Add Entities:	6	Click the first symbol icon, the rectangle. This is a fundamental entity.

7   Place the cursor in the middle of the diagram workspace and click the *left* mouse button. An entity is drawn.

8   Name the entity "Student Driver" and click OK.

9   Add another fundamental entity below the first, and name it "Driving School."

10   Add another fundamental entity below Driving School, and name it "Driving Lessons."

Figure 5-2 New Entities

Save the Diagram: 11   From the File menu, choose Save and name the diagram "Driving School View."

Changing a Symbol Type

In the diagram we have created, the entity Driving Lessons is actually an attributive entity because the entity exists solely because it is an attribute of the fundamental entity Driving School. Since we placed it on the diagram as a fundamental entity, it is necessary to change the symbol type.

Select Symbol to Change:	1	Put the cursor in selection mode by clicking the ↖ button on the control bar.
	2	Click the symbol labeled Driving Lessons with the *right* mouse button so that its **Object** menu appears.
Change the Entity Type:	3	Select **Change Item**. The Scope must be set to Global change in the **Change Object** dialog box. This option is important when you change an object's type or label. Selecting Global causes the change to be made on every diagram where that object occurs. If you select Individual, the change is only made to the selected object. A Local change would modify all occurrences on the current diagram. All changes to a symbol type must be Global.
	4	Select Change Type.
	5	Select Attributive Entity and click OK.
	6	Click OK on the **Change Object** dialog box. The symbol is changed on the diagram.

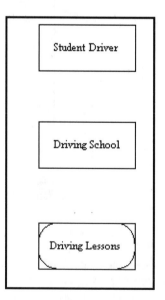

Figure 5-3 Changed Entity Type

Adding Relationship Lines

We need to establish the relationships between the entities on the current diagram.

Draw the 1 Click the first line button on the control bar.
Relationship:

2 Draw a line from Driving School to Student Driver. The procedure is the same as that used to draw a line in Lesson 2 - Diagramming. Click and hold the *left* mouse button where you want the line to begin, drag the line to where you want it to end. If you release the button within the symbol, the line is connected automatically. If not, you must double-click the left mouse button to end the line.

Note
⬚ When you use an elbow line and the elbow in the line does not bend in the direction that you want it to, click the *right* mouse button while you are still holding the *left* one, and the elbow inverts.

Label the 3 Enter "Instructs" for the label of the first relationship. To
Relationship: set the relationship cardinality, click One for the Minimum, and click Many for the Maximum. This means that "Driving School instructs one or many Student Drivers." If you know the exact maximum number of relationships, you can enter it in the detail box. (See Figure 5-4.)

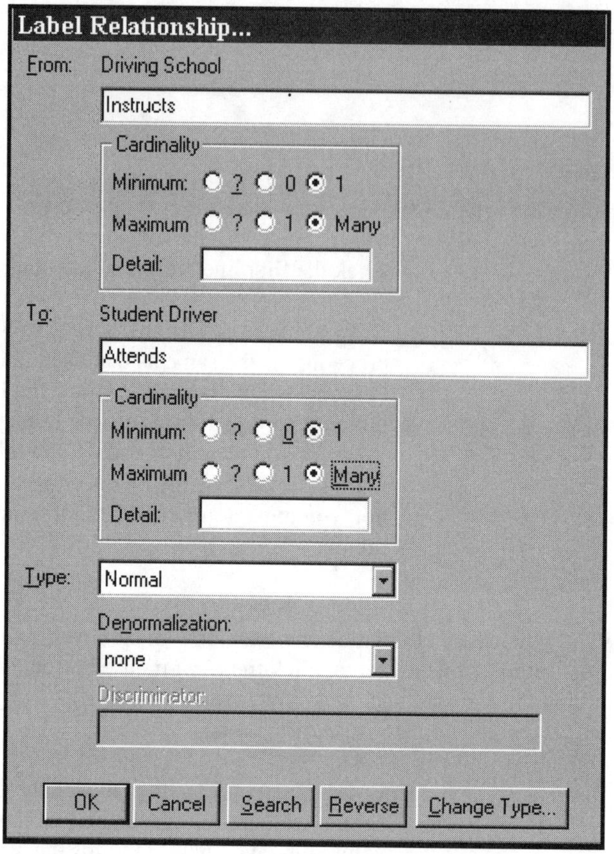

Figure 5-4 Label Relationship Dialog Box

4   Press the TAB key to move the cursor to the next field or
        click the mouse in the other label field.

5   Enter "Attends" for the reverse relationship name. For the
        Minimum click One, and for the Maximum click Many.
        (This deliberate error is added to demonstrate the
        capabilities of the Analyze function.) It means a "Student
        Driver attends one to many Driving School." Both of
        these relationships are considered mandatory because it is
        necessary to attend driving school to be a student driver,
        and it is necessary to have students to be a driving school.
        Ensure that Type is set to Normal, and click OK.

Draw Another Relationship:	6	Draw a line from Driving School to Driving Lessons. For the first label, type "Offers," and set Minimum to Zero and Maximum to Many. For the second label, type "Are Provided By." Because this is an Identifying relationship, the cardinality is automatically set to 1:1. Click OK.
Save:	7	Press CTRL+S to save the diagram.

Analyzing the Diagram

The Analyze function checks to ensure that the diagram is syntactically correct, meaning that all relationship lines and symbols are labeled. You can also use the Analyze function to check for certain normalization errors.

Start Analyze:	1	Select Analyze from the Diagram menu.
	2	Choose Current Diagram and Syntax Check. Click OK. It tells you that the current diagram is correct.
Insert an Error:	3	Add a symbol to the diagram without naming it.
Analyze Again:	4	Run Analyze again. You see an error message indicating that there is one unnamed entity. Click Cancel to return to the diagram. The unnamed entity can be deleted from the diagram by highlighting it with the cursor in selection mode and pressing Delete.
Analyze Still Again:	5	Run Analyze again, but this time choose Normalization. You see the error message that the relationship "Driving School [Instructs] Student Driver" is not normalized. This is true. The error indicates that the cardinality is 0:many or many:many in both directions. It is flagged as an error because optional:optional and many:many relationships can be difficult to implement. Click Cancel to close the box.
Correct Cardinality Error:	6	To change the cardinality of the relationship Attends, click the relationship line with the *right* button.
	7	Select Change Item. Change the cardinality for Attends from a maximum of Many to a maximum of One.

8   Click OK.

Analyze Once More: 9   Select Analyze from the Diagram menu. Choose
Normalization and click OK. The diagram is now correct.

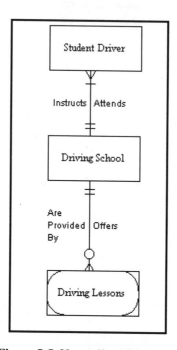

Figure 5-5 Normalized Diagram

Automatically Generating a View of Your Data Model

Another very useful feature of Visible Analyst is the ability to generate new data model views automatically. Since a data model can become very large and sometimes very difficult to decipher with many relationship lines and symbols, generating a specific view of the data model allows you to focus on one portion of your data model without having to redraw all of the symbols and connections that you want to have on the diagram. The function for generating a view is found on the View of Data Model submenu from the File menu.

There are three different options for generating a view from this function.

- There is an option to generate a global view of your data model. All of the entities and relationships that are in the repository are placed on one diagram. This feature is important when additions are made to one portion of the data model and you would like to see how those changes have affected the entire model. Another use for this feature is to generate an entity relationship diagram for imported entity information.

- You can generate a new view, allowing you to choose from the entities you have already created on a diagram or in the repository those entities and attached relationships you would like displayed on a new diagram. This allows you to make additions or changes to your entire data model while concentrating on only one portion.

- The other view option from the View of Data Model option is Process. A process view is an entity relationship diagram that represents a subset of your data model and is based upon a process existing on a data flow diagram or in the repository. Data elements that enter or leave the selected process in data flows and that are also contained in the composition of entities cause those entities to appear in the process view, along with the relationships existing between pairs of entities. A process view allows you to concentrate on the specific portion of your data model that is involved with the selected process. This is the type of view that you now create. The composition information for the entities that appeared, as well as the attribute information of the particular process, has already been entered for you in the sample diagrams we supplied. This is so that you do not have to enter the information necessary to demonstrate this feature of Visible Analyst.

To create the process view:

Start View Generation: 1   Select View of Data Model from the File menu, then choose Process. The Select Process for Views dialog box appears.

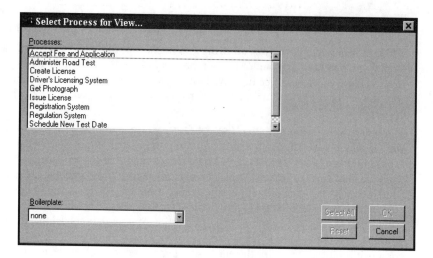

Figure 5-6 Process View Dialog Box

Select the Process: 2 Click the process Issue License and click OK. Visible Analyst searches the repository for entities that contain data elements in common with the data flows that are attached to Issue License and creates a "View" of the data model.

Save the New View: 3 Select **Save** from the **File** menu.

4 Title the diagram "Process View: Issue License." This diagram is a subset of your entire data model.

5 Click OK.

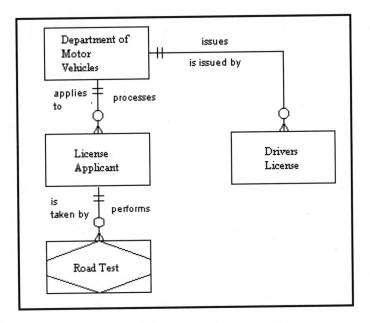

Figure 5-7 The Generated Process View

Lesson 6

Data Flow Diagrams

OVERVIEW

As described in Lesson 3 – Structured Modeling Techniques, a data flow diagram (DFD) is used for process modeling. This modeling technique shows the flow and transformation of the data without regard to the details of the data structure or type. It clearly represents where the transactions and transformations occur in your system.

A DFD is not the same as a flow chart, although there are certain similarities. A flow chart is much less specific with regard to how pieces of data are broken down, combined, and moved around the system than is a DFD. On the other hand, a flow chart is much more specific and physical than a DFD with regard to how processing is performed. A data flow diagram is more flexible and has a more general applicability than does a flow chart.

Data flow diagramming is not designed to show materials flow, just data. For example, if you were modeling a bookstore, how all of the receipts, invoices, inventory counts and financial transaction items are handled would be shown on your diagrams; but the books themselves would not. The books are materials, and their movement from the publisher to the store's loading dock to the shelves to the bag in the customer's hand is materials flow and not a part of data flow diagramming.

In any structured analysis methodology, the first task is to draw a top-level diagram, a simple summary of the overall system. It shows the system environment and major inputs and outputs, and is sometimes referred to as the basic problem statement. This is usually much less specific than the way most people picture a system because so many details are omitted. It should involve only one, two, or three processes and a very few external entities (source/sinks). In the example that follows, you use only one process and two source/sinks, though a top-level diagram could contain a few more of each. You break down (decompose) these top-level elements into more specific processes and flows. Some methodologies and analysts like to use a single process to represent the highest level of the data flow diagram. This is called a context diagram, and only one process is allowed on a context diagram to designate the entire system. For child diagrams, though, you can have multiple processes on any diagram.

The idea behind creating a general top-level diagram is twofold:

- To ensure agreement and understanding of the fundamental, overall mission of the system. There is confusion on this more often than is realized, and the details can rarely work well if the overall mission is unclear.

- To make explicit the source and derivation of the more detailed operations of the system. Often it is the second or third level of design that is the taken-for-granted starting point. Making the derivation explicit is important both for the design discipline itself and for the completeness of the resulting documentation. If you start Visible Analyst at the highest level, the tracking of all subsequent derivations automatically results from the data repository documentation.

There are four meaningful objects that appear on data flow diagrams:

Process
        The process symbol is accessed with the first symbol button on the control bar. If you are using Yourdon rules, a process is represented by a circle. For Gane & Sarson rules, a process is represented by a rounded-corner square. For SSADM and Mètrica rules, a process is represented by a square.

        A process signifies that something is happening to transform data. At the highest level you could show the whole bookstore as a single process.

        After creating the context (or high-level) diagram, you then break that diagram down into processes representing the various departments of the store, then into processes representing the functions of the departments, then into subdivisions of these processes, and so forth to as fine a level of description as you wish. This is done by "nesting" or decomposing a process and creating a child diagram at a greater level of detail, one that shows all of the inputs and outputs to the parent process and allows you to show what is going on inside it. Processes have numbers, and those numbers reflect the decomposition hierarchy, as shown in Figure 6-1.

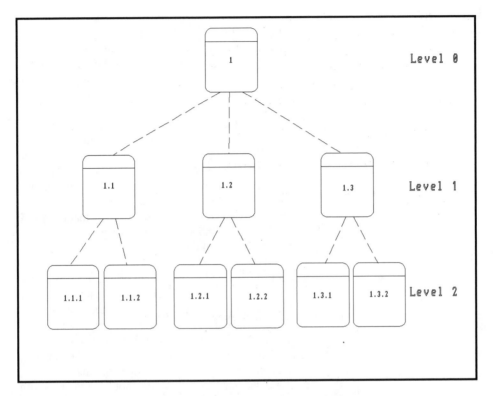

Figure 6-1 A Process Numbering Scheme

Data Store (or File)

A data store or file is accessed using the second symbol button on the control bar. If you are using Yourdon rules, a file is represented by two horizontal parallel lines. For Gane & Sarson, SSADM, and Mètrica rules, a data store is shown as a rectangle with the right side open; and it has a number. A data store is a place where data is kept while it is not actively being processed. Your process model does not show how it is stored, whether encoded on magnetic disk or scribbled on the back of an envelope, just that it is stored. Data can only enter a data store from a process and can only leave a data store to a process. The detailed data element in a data store can be defined in the Visible Analyst repository.

External Entity (or Source/Sink)

An external entity is accessed using the last symbol button on the control bar. It is represented by a large square under Yourdon rules; a square drawn with relief under Gane & Sarson rules; and an oval under SSADM and Mètrica rules. An external entity is something outside the boundary of the system you are modeling that either sends data to your system or receives data from it. It is effectively a black box, in that what happens inside the external entity is not material to your system description. It is only there to make clear some of the environment in which your system resides. External entities are optional. A net input data flow can just as well be shown coming from nowhere as from an external entity. Note that an external entity has no relation to the entity that is a part of entity relationship modeling. It is simply an unfortunate duplication of terminology.

Data Flow

A data flow depicts the movement of one to many items of data. Data can enter a system from outside, such as the entries that appear on a publisher's invoice or a packing list. (The invoice data flow is shown entering a process— it *must* enter a process—where it is examined and acted upon.) This process might send some of the data to be stored, some to be printed, some to be ignored. These invoice data elements may or may not be combined with elements from other input data flows and may then exit the process as parts of other data flows. To draw a data flow line, click on a line type in the control bar.

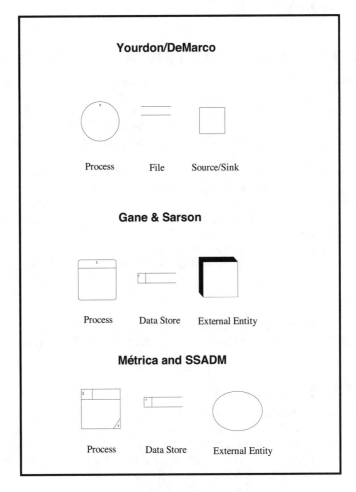

Figure 6-2 Data Flow Diagramming Symbols

Note

🗋 In Yourdon methodology, names of data flows contain hyphens instead of spaces. When you enter a space in a data flow name, the Visible Analyst automatically replaces the space with a hyphen.

This lesson leads you through the diagram creation process for a Gane & Sarson-based process model. Basic drawing and decomposing a process into a subordinate "child" diagram are shown. Also, you see how the system is validated using the rules capabilities of Visible Analyst. You build errors into your diagram to demonstrate the types of errors that can be identified by the Analyze function.

CREATING AND POPULATING A TOP-LEVEL DIAGRAM

The basic procedure for creating a top-level DFD is the same as creating a new diagram for the unstructured diagram type. The only difference is that if you choose a context diagram, by clicking the box at the bottom of the New Diagram screen, a process symbol number 0 is automatically placed on the diagram; and you are prompted for its name. A context diagram is permitted only one process symbol. You can add data flows and other symbols to the diagram.

This diagram has already been created for you so that you do not have to draw the diagrams and enter repository information. It is named DMV System and is shown in Figure 4-9, the top-level diagram of the DFDs you spawned from your FDD. This diagram also has one child diagram called Driver's Licensing System. You can display a list of diagrams by selecting Open Diagram from the File menu, or by clicking the Open button on the control bar. When a diagram type has a plus sign next to it, it means that diagrams of that type have been created. Click the plus sign to display the list of existing diagrams, then double-click the diagram you would like to open. (You can hide the list again by clicking the minus sign next to the diagram type name.)

To close a diagram, click the control button in the top left corner of the diagram window and select Close, double-click the control button, or choose Close Diagram from the File menu.

NESTING A PROCESS

In this unit, you structurally decompose a process symbol. This is also called "nesting" or "exploding" a process. The File menu contains the Nest function for this purpose; the submenu contains the Explode function. Explode can also be found by clicking the *right* mouse button on a process symbol that you want to model in more detail to display its Object menu, and then selecting Explode.

If the process has not previously been decomposed, this generates a "child" diagram from this "parent" process. All of the data flows attached to the parent process are automatically "dragged down" to the child diagram by the Nest function. These flows can be attached to the lower-level processes that you create on the child diagram. Those lower-level processes can then be nested further to increase the level of detail. In the current example, the child diagram was created by the Spawn function that you executed in Lesson 4 – Functional Decomposition Diagrams, and the processes you added to the FDD were placed on it.

Open the Diagram: 1   From the File menu or the open diagram button on the

Select a Process: 2

control bar, open the data flow diagram DMV System, if it is not still open from a previous lesson. This is the context diagram for this project.

Click the right mouse button on the process Driver's Licensing System to open its Object menu, and choose Explode. This opens the existing child diagram Driver's Licensing System and is an alternate way to navigate between the diagrams of your project, avoiding the File menu.

Explode It: 3

Click the *right* mouse button on the process labeled Issue License and choose Explode. The flows attached to the parent process are dragged down to the spawn-created diagram entitled Issue License, where the three process symbols from the functional decomposition diagram were placed. Maximize the diagram. The dragged-down flows are lined up on the sides of the child diagram, input flows on the left, output flows on the right. (See Figure 6-3.) Since you did not move the symbols on the diagram before nesting, it is possible that the dragged-down flows were drawn over a symbol.

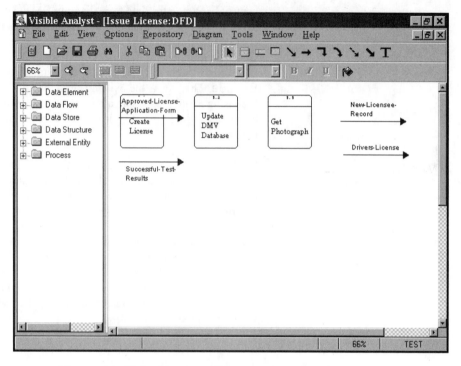

Figure 6-3 Child Diagram With Dragged-Down Flows

Edit the Diagram: 4   Move the symbols and attach the flows as shown in
Figure 6-4. To move a symbol, click and drag it with the
left mouse button. To attach the lines, click one endpoint.
Then click the *left* mouse button on the middle of the data
flow and drag the line so that it is positioned correctly.
When the data flow is selected, it changes color; and the
line becomes a dashed line as it is moved on the diagram.
Do the same for the other data flows. (Ignore for now the
other flows you see in Figure 6-4; you add them later in
this section.)

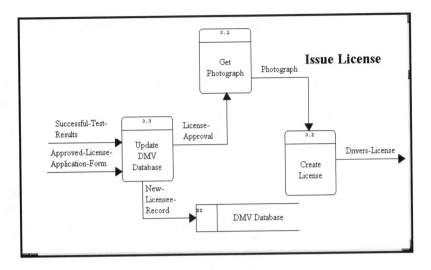

Figure 6-4 The Completed Diagram

Note

☐   When you want to show a data flow line (or another type of line) as attached to a process (or another type of symbol), you must drag the end of the line into contact with the symbol. With the Auto Connect option on, Visible Analyst redraws your connection at the outer edge of the symbol.

Add Flows and Text: 5   Add two new data flows: License-Approval and Photograph. Since these are internal flows, as opposed to net input or net output data flows[7]appearing on the parent, the **Nest** function could not create them.

Change Line Format: 6   You may want to change the data flow lines from straight to elbow. This can be done by highlighting the line and then selecting **Line Settings** from the **Options** menu and changing the line orientation to elbow. Or click the elbow line button on the control bar before drawing the lines.

To change the orientation of an elbow, position the cursor over the line segment handle to change and click, but do not release, the left mouse button. Move the mouse slightly until the line changes from solid to dashed, and

---

[7]For a full explanation of net input and output flows, please see the Visible Analyst *Operation Manual* or the online help.

then press the right mouse button. Release the left mouse button to save the change.

7 Click the T button on the control bar to add the caption text "Issue License" to display the diagram title on the diagram. Note that there is a way to do this automatically by using boilerplates. You can read about this in the Visible Analyst *Operation Manual* or in the online help system. (Boilerplates are not available in the Education Editions of Visible Analyst.)

Add a File: 8 If you wish, you can add the file DMV Database to the diagram. Since it appears on the context diagram, this is not necessary, but some people feel that showing it on a lower-level diagram adds clarity. Move the flow New Licensee-Record to attach it to the file DMV Database. A symbol is considered attached to a line when the endpoint of the line is touching the edge of the symbol. (It does not automatically connect to the symbol.)

Save: 9 Select Save from the File menu.

CREATING A NEW DIAGRAM

In previous sections of this lesson, you worked with diagrams that were either supplied by Visible Systems or created by the Spawn function. In this unit, you create and populate a new diagram yourself and practice more data flow diagramming techniques. You structurally decompose the process Administer Road Test (drawing a level-three diagram) that details what occurs within the process Administer Road Test.

If you have any other diagrams open, you should maximize the window by clicking the Maximize button in the upper right corner of the window.

Set the Zoom Level: 1 Set the zoom level to 66% from the View menu.

Open the Parent Diagram: 2 Select Nest from the File menu.

3 Select Parent from the submenu. You move up the diagram tree to display the diagram Driver's Licensing System.

Nest a Process: 4 With the *left* mouse button, select the process symbol

Administer Road Test by clicking on it. It is highlighted as the current object.

5   From the File menu, select Nest and then Explode.

6   Choose Create New Diagram. If you had previously nested this process, the child diagram would have displayed automatically. This option is useful to drag down new data flows that you may have drawn on the parent diagram to child diagrams after the child diagram has been created. A new diagram is drawn with your input flows in the upper left corner of the diagram, and the output flows in the upper right corner. If you cannot see the flows, select 33% zoom from the View menu and your diagram, shown in Figure 6-5, scales down so that you can see more of it.

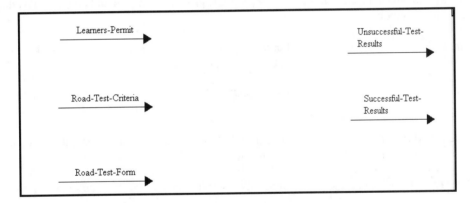

Figure 6-5 Exploded Diagram with Flows

Save: 7   Select Save from the File menu and click OK. The title of your diagram defaults to the name of the parent process. Visible Analyst indicates that it is saving *both* diagrams. This is because they are involved in a nest relationship and both ends of the nest relationship must be saved in the repository.

Adding Processes to a Child Diagram

Now add processes to the child diagram named Administer Road Test. The processes contained in this diagram are the individual processes that make up the parent process Administer Road Test. This diagram is a more detailed representation of the transformations and interactions that occur to the data flows within the parent process.

Add Processes:	1	Click the first symbol button, process, in the control bar.
	2	Add and label three processes: Validate Applicant, Test Vehicle Knowledge, and Test Driving Capabilities.
Save:	3	Select Save from the File menu.

Attaching Data Flows to Symbols

The input data flows on the left side of the diagram and the output data flows on the right side of the diagram were dragged down to the child diagram with the Nest function. It is necessary to attach the data flows to the appropriate processes on the child diagram. To attach a flow to a symbol:

Select a Line:	1	Put the cursor in selection mode by clicking the ↖ button on the control bar.
	2	Select the data flow Learners-Permit. The line handles appear.
Drag It Into Position:	3	Drag it to the edge of the process symbol labeled Validate Applicant, as shown in Figure 6-6.
Repeat for Other Flows:	4	Attach the other dragged-down flows as shown in Figure 6-6.
Add New Flows:	5	Click the first line button on the control bar.
	6	Add a flow from process Validate Applicant to Test Vehicle Knowledge and label it "Valid-Applicant."
	7	Click the straight line button on the control bar and add an input flow into the process Test Driving Capabilities and label it "Test-Criteria."

8   Add a flow from process Test Vehicle Knowledge to process Test Driving Capabilities, but leave it unlabeled by clicking Cancel or pressing ESC when you are prompted to enter a name. (This deliberate error is added to demonstrate the capabilities of the Analyze function.)

9   Add an unattached data flow labeled "Driving-Criteria." (Remember, you must double-click to end the line when it is not attached to a symbol.) This demonstrates the ability to select an existing flow from the diagram when a flow is split.

Save: 10   From the File menu select Save.

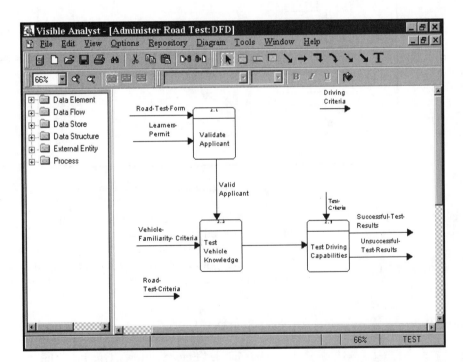

Figure 6-6 Child Diagram with Processes and Flows

Splitting Data Flows

Decomposing, or "splitting," a data flow offers the capability to divide net input or net output data flows into subflows, creating more detailed representation on lower-level diagrams. The concept is illustrated in Figure 6-7. This capability greatly aids in the system analysis process by showing more complex data flows at high levels of the structured specification and smaller or even atomic data flows at the lower levels of the structured specification. This decomposition capability provides a better understanding of the entire system and its parts. Whenever a dragged-down data flow is split into subflows, the original flow is erased from the current diagram and replaced by the selected or created subflows.

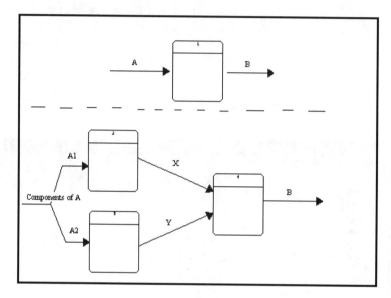

Figure 6-7 Splitting a Data Flow

Select a Flow to Split: 1   Click the ⬉ button on the control bar to put the cursor into selection mode.

2   Display the **Object** menu for the data flow labeled Road-Test-Criteria by clicking on one end of it with the *right* mouse button.

Start the Split: 3   Choose Split Data Flow.

4   In the box labeled Enter Subflows, type in "Vehicle-Familiarity-Criteria." This option draws a new flow (a subflow of Road-Test-Criteria) on the diagram with this label. See Figure 6-8. If you want to add more than one name in this box, press ENTER to place the cursor on a new line.

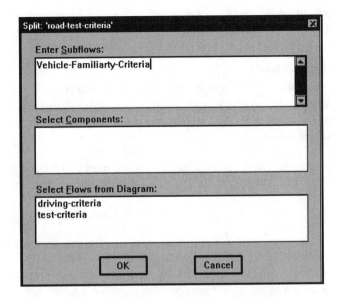

Figure 6-8 Split Data Flow Dialog Box

5   In the box marked Select Flows from Diagram, click
        Driving-Criteria. This option allows you to select an
        existing flow to be a subflow of Road-Test-Criteria.

6   Click OK. Notice that the flow Road-Test-Criteria is no
        longer on the diagram and that the flow Vehicle-
        Familiarity-Criteria has been added to the diagram.

7   Attach the flow Driving-Criteria to the process Test
        Driving Capabilities with the arrow pointing *away* from
        the process symbol. (This error is made deliberately; it is
        explained during the discussion of Analyze.)

8   Ignore the data flow Vehicle-Familiarity-Criteria, as
        another test for Analyze.

ANALYZING FOR BALANCE AND COMPLETENESS

As a project goes through a number of nested decompositions (nests), data flow splits, various
object moves and other edit procedures, there is a significant possibility that various data
flows are incorrectly used, or that objects are forgotten, etc. For a large project with many
symbols and flows, this is a real probability; and the errors are not easily detected by visually

checking the diagrams yourself. The **Analyze** function, found on the **Diagram** menu, is designed to warn you of completeness and logic errors. The function checks diagrams for:

- Labels on all objects.
- Unattached objects.
- At least one input flow and one output flow for each process.
- Data flow balance, which implies that an input flow is used everywhere as an input flow rather than an output flow and that data flows are properly accounted for at all levels of the diagram hierarchy.

The diagram is now analyzed for adherence to the rules of the Gane & Sarson methodology. Those rules are outlined in the Visible Analyst *Operation Manual* and in the online help.

| *Analyze the Diagram:* | 1 | Select **Analyze** from the **Diagram** menu. |
| | 2 | Select Current Diagram and click OK. |

Visible Analyst displays the errors found. To display the errors full screen, click the Maximize button in the upper right corner of the error window. If an error message extends beyond the box, use the scroll bar at the bottom of the box to scroll the text to the left. There should be five messages.

Data Flow labeled 'Vehicle-Familiarity-Criteria' is dangling.	This indicates that Vehicle-Familiarity-Criteria is not attached to a process.
There are 1 unnamed Data Flow(s).	This is the data flow that you left unlabeled on the diagram.
Net input Data Flow 'Test-Criteria' is not shown attached to parent Process.	This indicates that the data flow Test-Criteria has been added to the child diagram but is not accounted for on the parent diagram.
'Driving-Criteria' should be shown as a net input Data Flow.	This indicates that Driving-Criteria is being used as a net output flow on the diagram, while it is used as a net input flow on the parent.
Input Data Flow 'Road-Test-Criteria' on parent is not shown.	This message is a result of the fact that Vehicle-Familiarity-Criteria, a child flow of Road-Test-Criteria is not *attached* to a process as a net input flow, even though it appears on the diagram.

Note

⬜ Analysis error dialog boxes allow you to keep them on the screen while you carry on various Visible Analyst activities. This is to make it easier for you to correct the errors found by **Analyze**. If you don't want to keep the box open, press ESC or click Cancel to close it.

Fixing the Errors

Correct the Data Flows: 3   Attach the data flow Vehicle-Familiarity-Criteria to the process Test Vehicle Knowledge, as shown in Figure 6-9.

     4   Reverse the direction of Driving-Criteria, so that it becomes an input flow to Test Driving Capabilities (see Figure 6-9), by dragging the endpoints.

     5   Delete Test-Criteria by clicking on the line and pressing the DELETE key.

     6   Label the unlabeled data flow "Vehicle-Knowledge" by clicking on the line with the *right* mouse button and selecting **Change Item** from the **Object** menu. Then enter the label and click OK

Analyze Again: 7   Select **Analyze** from the **Diagram** menu again.

     8   Choose Current Diagram and click OK. The diagram should now be correct.

Note

⬜ It is unnecessary to save a diagram after **Analyze** has been performed because Visible Analyst automatically saves it for you before analysis begins.

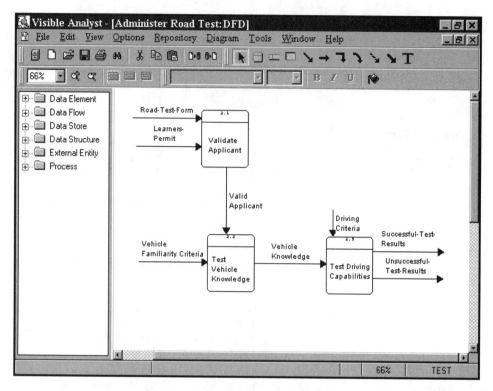

Figure 6-9 The Completed Diagram

GENERATING A PROCESS DECOMPOSITION MODEL

A process decomposition model for a process shows you the hierarchical structure of a decomposed process that has been nested.

Note

☐ A *process* decomposition diagram is very different from a *functional* decomposition diagram. The former is simply an unstructured diagram displaying the hierarchy of processes that are descendants of an indicated process. The latter, discussed in Lesson 4 -Functional Decomposition Diagrams, is a full diagramming methodology for performing business planning.

Open the Diagram:	1	From the Window menu, click "DMV System: DFD."
Select a Process:	2	Click the process Driver's Licensing System with the *right* mouse button.

Create the	3	Select Decompose. An unstructured diagram is generated
Decomposition:		showing the hierarchical structure of the process.
Save the New Diagram:	4	Select **Save** from the **File** menu. Label the diagram
		"Process Decomposition" and click OK.

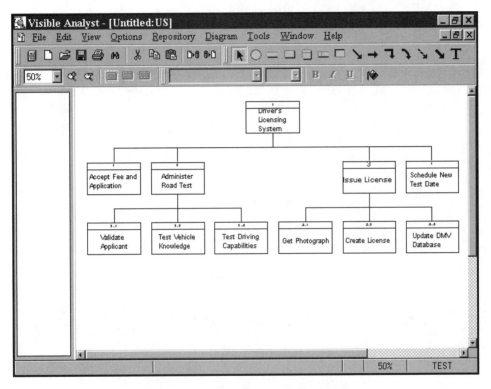

Figure 6-10 Process Decomposition Diagram

Lesson 7

Structured Design and Structure Charts

OVERVIEW

Structured design (SD) and structure charts (SC) produce the road map of how the new information application is built, tested and operated. SD and SC define modules, invocation sequences, control architectures, calling and return flows, decision logic, looping and other programmatic level operations. The structure chart is top-down, hierarchical in nature, and produces one overall diagram of the application. The repository entries for the modules can contain pseudo-code and detailed specifications for how the module performs its operations. Specifications for testing, test data and other project details can also be defined in the repository. In addition, the components from the data flow models and the data models can be reused to assure that all processes have been covered in the structured design and the defined database structures used to build the programmed data stores.

A key concept in structured design is to define, build and test clearly defined, limited function programming modules. These modules are easier to build and maintain, and they operate using a hierarchical control executive that manages the flow and control between modules. The use of standards for calling sequences, operational flows and parameter passing helps to maintain the consistency of the design logic and to make the application easier to build, test and maintain.

This unit leads you through the diagram creation process for a basic structure chart. Previous lessons acquainted you with the fundamental drawing techniques. Therefore, this unit is short and concentrates on drawing features unique to structure charts. You are also shown a different method of adding items to a diagram.

Definitions

A structure chart is the diagram used for structured design. The purpose of structured design is to provide a technique for transforming process descriptions and specifications generated using data flow diagramming into a design for a set of computer programs. As such, it is almost a graphical programming technique. Structured design is practiced in a more subjective manner than is structured analysis, meaning that there are fewer hard and fast rules for how a given project analysis should be transformed into a structured design. We lead you through a simple design process that produces a set of program design specifications. If code generation is part of your tool, we show you how to use Visible Analyst to generate shell code.

Unlike a data flow diagram, a structure chart is considered to be a single, possibly huge, diagram. For ease of viewing, parts of the structure chart are displayed on different pages. Modules can invoke modules on other pages of the chart, but all modules are conceptually on the same level. As an alternative to connecting many diagrams with page connectors, you could generate one large diagram using the multi-page option. (The multi-page option is not available in the Education Editions of Visible Analyst.)

There are only a few diagramming constructs used in structured design (Figure 7-1).

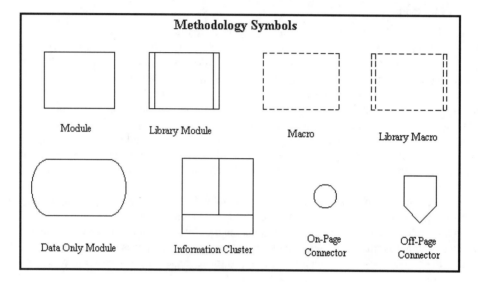

Figure 7-1 Structure Chart Diagramming Symbols

Module   A module symbolizes a package of instructions to carry out some operation, that is, a computer program or subroutine. They come in various forms (modules, library modules, macros, library macros), but they are all essentially capsules of instructions. There is a very loose relationship between the processes appearing in a process model and the modules appearing on a structure chart, in that the modules contain the code for performing the processes; but the correspondence is highly variable and subjective. The means of transforming one into the other is beyond the scope of this tutorial; please consult one of the texts on the subject referred to in Lesson 3 – Structured Modeling Techniques for details. A basic module is a rectangle with solid borders.

Library Module	This is a module that is executed in the same way each time it is invoked. It differs in usage from the standard module by the fact that its interfaces to other modules (if any) are hidden from the designer. It is represented as a rectangle with double lines on the two vertical sides.
Macro	A macro is a module whose body is effectively copied in-line during translation (that is, compilation or assembly) as a result of being invoked by name. The only practical difference between a macro and a module is that macros tend to make a system operate faster, but at the expense of more memory space required to operate the system. A macro is represented as a rectangle with dashed sides.
Library Macro	This is a macro that is repeated in a system. It is a rectangle with dashed lines and double lines for the vertical sides.
Data Only Module	A data only module is simply a collection of data, analogous to a data store or a common area. This kind of module cannot be invoked since it contains no instructions, only data. The data can be shown being used by one or more modules. It is represented as a rectangle with rounded, convex sides.
Information Cluster	An information cluster is an aggregate symbol, a combination of two or more modules and a data only module that the modules share in common. You can tell Visible Analyst how many modules you want in your information cluster when you label it, and Visible Analyst draws the symbol appropriately.
On-Page Connector	To avoid crossing lines on a diagram, it is often convenient to begin an invocation on one part of a diagram and complete it discontinuously on another part. For this, the on-page connector is used. The on-page connector symbol is a small circle.
Off-Page Connector	A structure chart is viewed by Visible Analyst as one unified diagram. You can, however, spread your chart over multiple pages by linking them using invocations that begin on one page and end on another. The off-page connector symbol is identical in appearance to the page connector for FDDs.

Invocation Line

An invocation is a line drawn from one module to another showing that the first module invokes (or calls) the second, with the implication that control will eventually return to the invoking module. The line is usually, but not always, drawn with an arrowhead terminator pointing to the invoked module. There are two variants of the invocation line called the control connection and the data connection.

Control Connection

A control connection describes a one-way transfer of control between modules. It is drawn as a line with a filled in circle on one endpoint and an arrowhead on the other. The arrowhead is optional.

Data Connection

A data connection depicts the passing of data between a module and a data only module. It is a line with an open circle on one endpoint and an arrowhead on the other. The arrowhead is optional.

Couple

A couple is a piece of information passed between modules and symbolizes the arguments passed between computer programs or functions. It is shown next to an invocation line, pointing in the direction in which it is passed. There are data couples, control couples, and generic couples.

A *data couple* represents data parameters that are passed between program modules. It is a short line with an *open* circle at one end and an arrow at the other.

A *control couple* represents information pertaining to the way modules function rather than the data on which they function. It is a short line with a *filled* circle at one end and an arrow at the other.

A *generic couple* shows that both data and control are passed between modules upon invocation. It is a short line with no circle at one end and an arrow at the other

Interface Table Row (ITR)

An interface table row represents a set of couples and is used to make complex diagrams more clear. The same symbols that are used for data, control, and generic couples are used to denote an ITR for that couple type. An ITR is drawn on a diagram in the same manner as a couple. Then the type of the line is changed to an ITR in the repository in the entry type field and the couples to be contained in the ITR are listed in the composition field of its repository entry.

Loop Line   The loop line type is the open ellipse shape shown in Figure 7-2. Even though it is a line, it cannot be labeled and cannot be defined in the repository. Its purpose is to show that an invocation line (of any type) is part of an iterative and/or an ordered set of invocations. In usage, a loop can be drawn around the start point of one or more invocation lines. Loops can be nested.

DRAWING A STRUCTURE CHART

Adding Symbols

Since you are already familiar with adding symbols, the description for this section is brief.

Create a New Diagram: 1   Select **New Diagram** from the **File** menu and choose Structure Chart.

Maximize the Diagram: 2   Maximize the workspace by clicking on the Maximize button in the top right corner of the window.

Set Zoom Level: 3   Set zoom level from the **View** menu to 66%.

Add Symbols: 4   Add the symbols to the diagram as shown in Figure 7-2.

Save: 5   Select **Save** from the **File** menu. Name the diagram "Menu Structure."

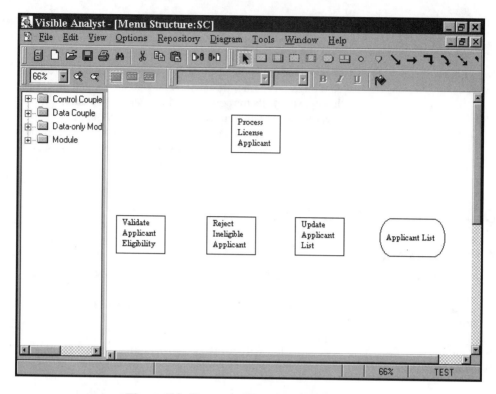

Figure 7-2 Structure Chart with Symbols

Adding Invocation Lines to a Structure Chart

The method for adding lines to a diagram is the same for all diagram types. This section reviews the line-adding procedure and also explains how to use different line terminators and line types. For any line that you create on a diagram, you can change its type immediately by selecting Line Settings from the Options menu while the line is still selected (highlighted). This gives you the ability to draw a line and then set the terminators. In this section, though, when it is necessary to draw a different type of line, you change the line type before you draw the line.

Draw an Invocation: 1   Click the first line type and position the cursor over the bottom line of the module Process License Applicant. Click and hold the *left* mouse button, and drag the line to the top of the module Validate Applicant Eligibility.

| | 2 | Release the mouse button within the symbol. (If Auto Connect is turned off, you must double-click to end the line.) This ends the line, and the line terminator is drawn. |

Deselect the New Line: 3 Open the **Diagram** menu. Note that the **Lines** menu item is checked, indicating that you are in line entry mode. If you were to click **Lines**, you would return to selection mode. This same type of action works for getting out of caption text modes. For symbol mode, you must click the selected symbol on the submenu.

4 You should still be in line adding mode. Click on an empty space on the diagram, so that the line you drew is no longer selected. (If you don't deselect the line, making changes in **Line Settings** affects the *selected* line, not a *future* line, as you want to do in this case.)

Change the Terminator Type: 5 Select **Line Settings** from the **Options** menu.

6 Select Decision as the Terminator Type and click OK.

Draw Conditional Invocations: 7 Draw an invocation line from Process License Applicant to Reject Ineligible Applicant. The line has a conditional terminator at the starting point of the line.

8 Click the *left* mouse button on the conditional terminator of the invocation you just drew and draw a line from Process License Applicant to Update Applicant List. The conditional terminator of the new invocation can be overlaid on top of the previous one, so that they appear as one binary choice. (Since the two invocations are in fact distinct, they can later be separated, if you want to display them as independent choices.) This establishes another conditional invocation relationship. It means that under certain circumstances, either Reject Ineligible Applicant is invoked or Update Applicant List is invoked. In this case, the circumstances depend upon whether or not the Applicant is valid.

9 Deselect the line.

Draw a Data Connection:	10	Select **Line Settings** from the **Options** menu.
	11	Select the Line Type to be Data Connection and the Terminator Type to be Single Arrow. Click OK.
	12	Draw a line between Update Applicant List and the data only module Applicant List. Then deselect the line.
Draw a Loop Line:	13	Select **Line Settings** from the **Options** menu.
	14	Select the Line Type to be Loop and click OK.
	15	You want to end up with a loop line like that shown at the bottom of the module Process License Applicant in Figure 7-3. Place your cursor on the edge of the module near the lower left corner. Click and drag the line so that its endpoint is at the lower right edge of the symbol and double click to complete the line. While the line is still selected, notice its handles. You can drag these around to change the shape and size of the loop.
Save:	16	Select **Save** from the **File** menu.

Drawing Couples

Enter Couple Mode:	1	Deselect the line.
	2	Select **Line Settings** from the **Options** menu.
	3	Select the Line Type to be Data Couple and click OK.

Note

⬜ When the cursor is over the drawing area, it displays as the couple-adding cursor. On any cursor there is a spot, called the "hot spot," that is the business end of the cursor; that is, the location at which you want some action to take place. For the couple-adding cursor, the hot spot is at the point of the large arrow at the top of the cursor.

Select the Invocation:	4	Click on either end of the invocation line between Process License Applicant and Validate Applicant Eligibility. This selects the line.

Draw the Couple:	5	Click on the start point of that line. A data couple is drawn pointing in the direction the data is passed. By clicking at the start of the invocation line, you indicated that the data couple is passed from Process License Applicant and follows the direction of the invocation line.
	6	Name the couple "Applicant Name" and click OK.
Draw More Couples:	7	Now that you know how to enter diagram objects using the **Diagram** menu, you can continue doing it the easy way using the tool bar buttons. Click on the couple with a filled circle (the last line button). This is a control couple. (You may have to click on the "gripper" to drag more of the diagram tools tool bar into view.)
	8	While it is still selected, click on the endpoint of the same invocation line where it meets Validate Applicant Eligibility. Name the new control couple "Applicant Valid" and click OK.
	9	Click on the second to the last line button, the data couple.
	10	Click on one end of the invocation line between Process License Applicant and Update Applicant List. This selects the line.
	11	Click on the endpoint of that line, where the terminator is attached to Update Applicant List. Name the data couple "Applicant Information."
Invert the Couple:	12	Look at Figure 7-3. If the couple you just drew is facing the wrong direction, it is easy to fix. To select the couple you just drew, press ESC to activate selection mode and click on the couple with the *right* mouse button.
	13	Choose **Change Item** from the **Object** menu, click the Invert Couple box, and click OK. The couple and its label move to the other side of the invocation.
Complete the Diagram:	14	Draw the other couples as shown in Figure 7-3.

Save: 15 Choose Save from the File menu to save the diagram. Your structure chart is complete.

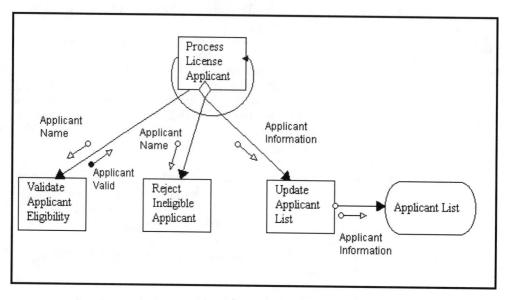

Figure 7-3 The Completed Structure Chart

Lesson 8
The Class Diagrams

OVERVIEW

Visible Analyst provides a series of capabilities for supporting the definition of object classes and a variety of object relationships and methods. Visible Analyst implements the concepts of Object Modeling and Design (OMT), as developed by Rumbaugh, et al, for the General Electric Company, and Rational's Unified Modeling Language (UML). These methods are similar, so they are covered together here.

The key to object modeling is the development of class diagrams that show the object elements and relationships, including cardinality, attributes, association, inheritance, and aggregation. There is considerable flexibility in these concepts to allow the user to define and implement a number of variations and options in the object model.

Visible Analyst's object modeling approach is implemented in a way that is very similar to the entity relationship model. A rectangular symbol is used to represent both a data entity and a class object. The relationship and cardinality questioning sequence is similar. Attributes of both entities and classes are displayed in similar formats. The key differences are in the extended definitions of the object in the Visible repository.

The object model is represented by class diagrams (CLDs) that contain classes, with an object being an instance of a class. The relationships between the classes for a project are depicted with lines and symbols to depict inheritance and aggregation. Like the ERD, the CLD can be built into views that show all or a subset of the classes and their relationships.

Definitions

The components of the class modeling process include:

Aggregation	An aggregation is a relationship that indicates the parent class contains the child.
Attributes	Attributes are data members describing the class object. An attribute can be assigned a name, class type, limit, type of visibility, reference method and a qualification flag indicating whether it is static or volatile.

Class	A class is a group of objects with the same data structure (attributes) and behavior (operations). A class is an abstraction that describes properties that are important to an application.
Inheritance	Inheritance is the sharing of attributes and operations among classes based on a hierarchical (parent and child) relationship.
Instance	Instance is a specific object from a class. Each instance of the class has its own value for each attribute but shares the attribute names and operations with other instances of the class.
Method	A method is a specific implementation of an operation by a certain class.
Operation	An operation is an action or transformation that an object performs or is subject to.
Relationship	The relationships between classes can define cardinality of classes (numeric relationships), aggregations, and inheritance. Refer to Adding Relationships to a View later in this chapter for a discussion of relationship attributes.
Subtype	Subtype provides additional information on how a class is used. A *Standard* class (the default) indicates a normal class. *Elemental* indicates the class contains no attributes and physical characteristics should be defined. *Structure* and *Union* subtypes indicate C type components should be used instead of a class. *Entity*, *Associative,* and *Attributive* indicate the class is persistent and can be used on an Entity Relationship Diagram.
Symbols	The symbols for a class diagram consist of rectangles that are defined as classes.
Visibility	Indicates the level of exposure to the outside world permitted by the class. The options are: public, private or protected.

DEVELOPING YOUR CLASS MODEL

Each class diagram is complete in and of itself and shows one view of the classes in your project. You begin your class model by specifying and defining classes of objects on a diagram and then establishing a definition of the relationships between the classes. You can also define the attributes and operations for the classes within the Visible Analyst repository.

Once you defined a class diagram, you can create additional views by selecting the File menu New Diagram function and choosing the New View Drawing Method. This selects existing class entities and relationships from the repository, and Visible Analyst automatically draws the views for you. You can add or subtract elements from each view and rearrange it as you wish. This allows you to establish object models for various portions of your project without having to create redundant definitions or large confusing diagrams. Any new objects or relationships created on any view are automatically updated into the Visible Analyst repository.

Adding Classes to a View

The basic building blocks of the class model are classes of objects that exist within an application. You begin the CLD with a new diagram and add and define classes to this view. For the lesson exercise, we return to the Department of Motor Vehicles application and concentrate on the Registration portion of the application.

Set the Zoom Level:	1	From the View menu, select 66% zoom so that you can see all of your needed workspace.
Create a New Diagram:	2	From the File menu select New Diagram.
	3	Select the diagram type Class.
	4	Select Standard Workspace and Landscape Orientation.
	5	Click OK.
Add Classes:	6	Click the class symbol button on the diagram tools tool bar.
	7	Place the cursor in the middle of the diagram workspace and click the left mouse button. A class object symbol is drawn.
	8	Name the Class symbol "Registrations."
	9	Add another class below Registrations, and name it "Trailers."
	10	Add another class below Registrations and name it "Vehicles."
	11	Add a class below Vehicles and name it "Trucks."

12   While trucks is still selected, click the right mouse button to display the Object menu, then select Stylize. Change the horizontal and vertical sizes to 75%. Click Apply, then click Set Default Size. Click OK.

13   Below Vehicles, add two more classes: Cars and Motorcycles.

14   To the right and slightly under Vehicles, create four more classes: Engine, Axles, Fuel, and Weight.

Save the Diagram: 15   From the File menu, choose Save and name the diagram "Registration Object Classes."

Reset Default Object Size: 16   Click on the Registrations object.

17   Select Stylize from the Diagram menu. Change the horizontal and vertical sizes to 100%. Click Apply, then click Set Default Size. Click OK.

Adding Relationships To A View

The relationships between classes establish the cardinality, aggregations or inheritance connections between the classes.

Drawing Relationships: 1   Click the first line choice on the diagram tool bar. This establishes a normal relationship between the classes. (Because the first line type icon is selected, the default cardinality is 1:1 and 1:1.)

2   Draw a line from Registrations to Vehicles. This procedure is the same as that used to draw an Entity Relationship Diagram in Lesson 5. Click and hold the left mouse button where you want the line to begin, and drag the line to the symbol where you want it to end.

3   Type "identify" for the label of the first relationship.

4   Use the TAB key to move to the next relationship label. Type "are licensed by" for the label that establishes the relationship of the vehicle to the registration. Click OK.

5   Draw a similar relationship between Registrations and Trailers. Use the same labels as you did for Registrations and Vehicles.

6   Select the line type for Inheritance, the fourth line button, and make connections between Vehicles and Trucks, Cars and Motorcycles. Start drawing the line at the same point on the class Vehicles so that the lines are overlaid as shown in Figure 8-1. The default label "is a" is automatically entered. You can change this or just click OK.

7   Select the line type for Aggregations and make the connections between Vehicles and Engines, Axles, Fuel and Weight. Start drawing the line at the same point on the class Vehicles so that the lines are overlaid. (When drawing a line over an existing line, the new line is red, indicating the lines are overlaid.) Use the labels "have," "use," "have," and "have," respectively, from Vehicles to these classes.

Save: 8   From the **File** menu choose **Save**. Your diagram should be similar to the one shown in Figure 8-1.

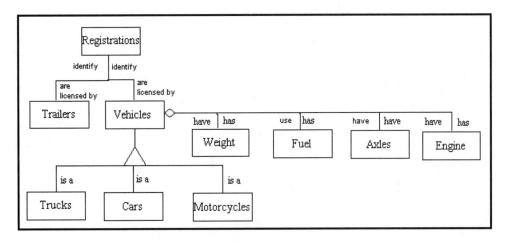

Figure 8-1 Class Relationship Notation

The information that is maintained for a relationship is:

- **From**. The name of the parent entity or class

- **Cardinality**. How many instances of one entity or class relate to another. The Detail field can be used to store a specific quantity, for example 1, 3 or 5+

- **To.** The name of the child entity or class.

- **Type.** The type of relationship. An *aggregation* relationship indicates the parent class contains the child. An *inheritance* relationship indicates the definition of the To class is based on the From class. The base class contains the basic definition, while the derived class implements only those features that need to be different. A *normal* relationship indicates there are no special characteristics between the objects involved.

- **Role.** The role names used for the parent and child classes. For normal relationships, a role should exist as an attribute of the class at the other end of the association with the Reference type set to Address. For aggregation relationships, it should be set to Value. The Visibility in both cases should be Protected, and the type set to the opposite class.

- **Qualifier.** The qualifier names used for the parent and child classes. If a qualifier is used, an attribute of type Void is created in the class at the other end of the association with the Reference type set to Address and the Visibility set to Protected. You can change the type of the qualifier by modifying the attributes field in the repository.

- **Ordered.** Ordering indicates the objects on the many side of a relationship have an explicit order. The term set is commonly used to describe an unordered association, while a list indicates an ordered association.

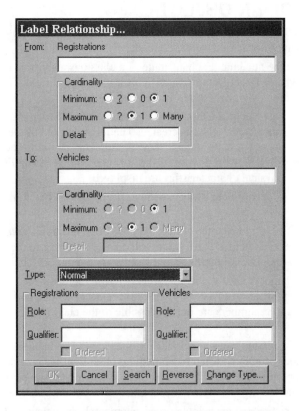

Figure 8-2 Labeling Relationship for DMV

Note

Each relationship between two entities or classes is a unique object in the repository. The fact that two relationships between two different pairs of objects may have the same name does not change the fact that the individual relationships are distinct. When using the Search function to name relationships, you are only selecting a *name*, not a *relationship repository object*. If, when you are finished, a pair of objects on this view is connected by relationships with the same names as relationships joining the same object on another view in the data or object model, then both sets of relationships are considered two different instances (locations) of the same repository object.

ATTRIBUTES OF AN OBJECT

Class objects are defined by their data members that can be selected in the Visible Analyst repository. The following information can be defined:

- **Name**. The name of the attribute. Each attribute of a class has a separate entry in the repository with a type of Local Data Element. This is an optional field. The Search button can be used to find other Member Names in the repository.

- **Type**. The attribute type can be a Class, Data Element, or Data Structure. If the type does not exist in the repository, a new class is created. The location field of the attribute type will contain a reference to the current class. This is a mandatory field. The Search button can be used to display a list of valid types. If the attribute type is a Data Element or Elemental Class, its physical characteristics are displayed.

- **Limit**. The number of occurrences of the attribute. If this field is blank, the attribute occurs once.

- **Reference**. A qualifier to indicate the access method for an attribute. *Value* indicates the object defined in the *Type* field is used; *Address* indicates a pointer to the object is to be used; and *Reference* indicates a reference to the object is to be used. The default is Value.

- **Visibility**. *Public* members have global visibility. *Private* members are only accessible to member functions and friends. *Protected* members are accessible to derived classes and friends. *Implementation* members are only accessible to the class itself. The default is Private.

- **Qualification**. *Constant* indicates a member's value cannot be changed. *Volatile* indicates the member can be modified by something other than the program, either the operating system or hardware. *Static* indicates there is only one instance of the member regardless of the number times a class is instantiated. The default is None.

- **Physical Characteristics**. If the attribute type is elemental, the physical characteristics can be set.

For every item entered into the Type field, Visible Analyst creates a repository entry (if one with the same name does not already exist) and updates that entry's location field. Likewise, if an item is removed from this field, that entry's location field is updated to reflect this. These repository entries are generally created as classes unless a data element already exists with the same name or the physical characteristics are defined.

As you enter items, the dialog box automatically scrolls as necessary to allow you to enter more items until you have finished. Insert is used to insert a new attribute into the list at the current position, while Delete removes the current attribute (the current position is indicated by ➤➤). When you have completed the entries, click OK to add them to the Attributes field.

Item names entered into this field may contain up to 128 characters each and may consist of any upper or lower case letters, numbers, spaces, periods, underscore characters and hyphens; but the first character must always be a letter.

Adding Attributes to a Class Diagram

Bring your Registration Class Objects CLD to the working diagram position and follow these steps:

Move to the Repository:	1	Select the Registrations class object and double-click the left mouse button to go to its repository entry.
Enter the Attributes Field:	2	Move the entry cursor to the Attributes field.
Bring Up Attributes Entry:	3	Click the Attributes Details button [icon] or select Add/Change from the Repository Object menu that is displayed when you right-click in the Attributes field.
Define Attributes:	4	Type attributes for the Registrations class object, as shown in Figure 8-3.
	5	Click OK to save your entries and return to the Define dialog box. Note that the attributes you entered are displayed in the Attributes field. Click Save and Exit to return to the diagram.

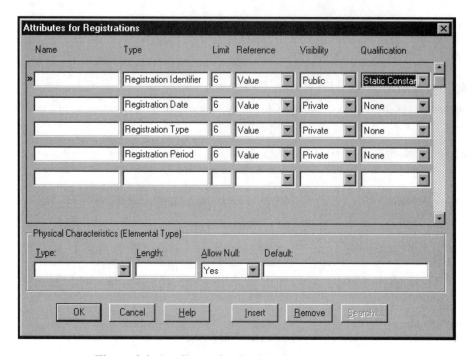

Figure 8-3 Attributes for Registration Class Object

Define More   6   Select the Trailers class object and double-click the left
Attributes: mouse button to go to its repository entry.

                       7   Move the entry cursor to the Attributes field.

                       8   Click the Attributes Details button, and complete the
                                  Attributes dialog box.   Type "Weight number" in the
                                  Type field, type "1" in the Limit field. Select Value in the
                                  Reference area, Public in the Visibility area, and None in
                                  the Qualification area.

                       9   Click OK to save your entries and return to the Define
                                  dialog box. Click Save, then click Exit to return to your
                                  diagram.

                      10   Double-click the left mouse button on the Vehicles class
                                  object to display its repository entry.

	11	Right-click in the Attributes field and select Add/Change from the Object menu that is displayed.
	12	Complete the Attributes dialog box by typing "Motor number" in the Type field, and "1" in the Limit field. Select Value in the Reference area, Public in the Visibility area, and None in the Qualification area.
	13	Click OK to save your entries and return to the Define dialog box. Click Save, then Exit to return to your diagram.
Complete Your Attributes:	14	Continue adding attributes to the remaining class objects on your diagram.
Exit the Define Dialog Box	15	When you have completed adding attributes to class objects, click Exit to close the Define dialog box.

METHODS FOR AN OBJECT

Methods are the operations defined for accessing a class. The methods are specified in the Visible Analyst repository and include the following information:

- **Returns.** The return type can be a Class or Data Element. If the type does not exist in the repository, a new class is created. The location field of the attribute type contains a reference to the method. This is an optional field. The Search button can be used to display a list of valid types.

- **Limit.** The number or size of the parameter. If this field is blank, it occurs once.

- **By.** A qualifier to indicate how the return value is passed. *Value* indicates a copy of the parameter is passed; *Address* indicates a pointer to the object is to be used; and *Reference* indicates a reference to an object is to be used.

- **Visibility.** *Public* methods have global visibility. *Private* methods are only accessible to other member functions within the same class and friends. *Protected* methods are accessible to derived classes and friends. *Implementation* methods are only accessible to the class itself. The default is Public.

- **Qualification**. *Static* indicates a method can be used without a specific instance of an object (it can only be used with static attributes (data members)). A *Virtual* method is one that you expect to be redefined in a derived class. A pure *Virtual* method has no definition and must be defined in a derived class. A class with any pure virtual functions is an abstract (or virtual) class. The default is None.

- **Arguments**. A list of parameters to be used by the method. This is an optional field. If a method appears more than once with the same name within a class, it must have a different argument list for each definition. This is known as function overloading. See the next section for defining arguments.

When a method is added to a class definition, an entry of type Module is created in the repository. The long name includes the class name and the argument list. The argument list is needed to differentiate between overloaded functions.

Note

☐ Because the same name can be used for more than one method, there may be duplicate Module entries in the repository, each belonging to a different class.

Arguments for Methods

When defining methods (member functions) for a class, the parameters to the function need to be specified. To add, change, or remove arguments, click the Arguments button on the Method Definition dialog box. For each argument, the following information can be defined:

- **Name**. The name of the parameter. This is an optional field.
- **Type**. The parameter type can be class or data element. If the type does not exist in the repository, a new class is created. This is a mandatory field. The Search button can be used to display a list of valid types. If the parameter type is a data element or elemental class, its physical characteristics are displayed.
- **Limit**. The number or size of the parameter. If this field is blank, it occurs once.
- **Pass By**. A qualifier to indicate the how the parameter is passed. *Value* indicates a copy of the parameter is passed; *Address* indicates a pointer to the object is used; and *Reference* indicates a reference to an object is used. The default is Value.
- **Qualification**. *Constant* indicates a parameter's value cannot be changed. *Volatile* indicates the parameter can be modified by something other than the program, either the operating system or hardware. The default is None.
- **Physical Characteristics**. If the parameter type is elemental, the physical characteristics can be set.

For every item entered into the Type field, Visible Analyst creates a repository entry (if one with the same name does not already exist). These repository entries are generally created as classes unless a data element already exists with the same name or the physical characteristics are defined.

As you enter items, the dialog box automatically scrolls as necessary to allow you to enter more items until you have finished. Insert is used to insert a new parameter into the list at the current position, while Delete removes the current parameter (the current position is indicated by ➤➤). When you have completed the entries, click OK to update the method name field.

Item names entered into this field may contain up to 128 characters each and may consist of any upper or lower case letters, numbers, spaces, periods, underscore characters and hyphens; but the first character must always be a letter.

Adding Methods to a Class Diagram

Methods are defined in the Visible Analyst repository. Bring the "Registration Class Objects" CLD to the working diagram position and follow these steps:

Move to Repository: 1 Select the class object "Registrations" and double-click the left mouse button to go to its repository entry.

Methods Window: 2 Move to the third page of the repository dialog box by clicking the Methods/Friends tab.

3 Move the cursor to the Methods field.

4 Click the Attributes Details button or select Add/Change from the Repository Object menu that is displayed when you right-click in the Methods field.

Enter Methods: 5 Define methods for the Registration. To do this, click the New button to name the new method "Registration Renewal," and click OK. Type "Data Element" in the Returns field, and "6" in the Limit field. Select Value in the By area, Public in the Visibility area, and None in the Qualification area. (Refer to Figure 8-4.) Repeat this process for new methods "Create New Registration" and "Suspend Registration."

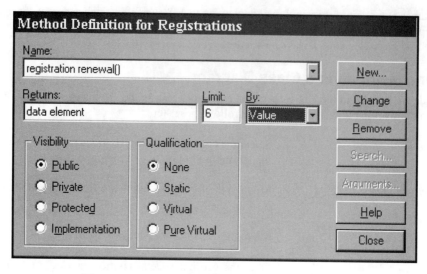

Figure 8-4 Method for Registration Object

6   Click Close to return to the Define dialog box.

7   Click Save, then Exit to return to your diagram.

Enter More Methods: 8   Double-click on the Trailers class object to display its repository entry, then click the Methods/Friends tab.

9   Click the Attributes Details button to display the Methods Definition dialog box.

10   Click the New button, and type "Weight Specification" in the Name field. Click OK.

11   Type "Data Element" in the Returns field, and type "1" in the Limit field. Select Reference in the By area, Public in the Visibility area and None in the Qualification area.

12   Click Close to return to the Define dialog box.

13   Click Save, then Exit to return to your diagram.

14   Select Vehicles, then right-click to display its Object menu.

15   Select Define to display its repository entry.

16   Click the Methods/Friends tab and put the cursor in the Methods box.

17   Right-click to display the Object menu, and select Add/Change to display the Method Definition dialog box.

18   Click the New button and name the new method "Motor Number Specification." Click OK.

19   Type "Data Element" in the Returns field and "1" in the Limit field. Select Reference in the By area, Public in the Visibility area, and None in the Qualifications area. Click Close.

20   Click Save, then Exit to return to your diagram.

Note

⬚   The attributes and/or methods for an object can be displayed on object model diagrams. This is done by making the appropriate selection of items to display from the View menu Class options window.

ANALYZING THE CLASS DIAGRAM

The Analyze function evaluates the following conditions of a class diagram.

- **Syntax errors.** These are errors that would make your class diagram impossible for Visible Analyst to understand.
- **Connection errors.** These indicate classes are improperly associated with other classes. Different rules apply depending on whether the relationship type is normal, inheritance or aggregation.
- **Use errors.** These indicate classes have not been used, either on a diagram or in the definition of another class.
- **Definition errors.** These indicate a class definition is incomplete; attributes or methods have not been defined. Different rules apply depending upon the class subtype.

Execute Analyze: 1   With your diagram for "Registration Class Objectives" in the active diagram window, select Analyze from the Diagram menu.

2   Review your error messages and decide an appropriate corrective step.

3   Save the diagram when finished.

Lesson 9

State Transition Diagramming

OVERVIEW

The state transition model defines the dynamic changes that occur in the life history of an object. The understanding of the different states and the conditions that trigger the changes from state to state represent the programmatic modules that must be built to allow the application to perform in harmony with the real world. State transition modeling consists of defining each stable state of an object and then defining the triggers or events that cause the object to change to another state. For example, an object "customer order" could be defined in states such as completed, back-ordered, partial, awaiting shipment, in-shipment, delivered, lost, overdue, billed-but-not-paid, paid partial, paid-in-full, etc. As the states are natural positions, and the events or triggers actions on the objects, the transitions from one state to another represent the operations modules of a system. In addition, the attributes that define the state condition are established and can be used to develop the triggers and event processes.

Definitions

The components of state transition modeling include:

State   The condition that an object can be at rest in. The state can be defined as a class of objects.

Triggers   The action or change of condition that will cause an object to change from one state to another.

Transitions   The steps that the object passes through in transition from one state to another.

Relationships

The relationship structure in a state transition diagram (STD) is directional arrows showing how an object moves from one state to another. The indication of the event triggers and the transition steps are outlined on the relationships.

DEVELOPING YOUR STATE TRANSITION MODEL

Each state transition model is composed of objects and provides a sequence of steps for each major transition within a project. The state transition model can be linked to the object class models using the nesting concept.

When beginning your state transition model you can enter the objects or nest down to the STD from a class diagram. For the lesson exercise, you develop the state transition model for the registrations in the DMV application. You use the definition that a registration can be in the following states:

- Never Registered (New Vehicle)
- Registered
- Unregistered
- Renewal Registration
- Registration Expired
- Vehicle Resold

These states and their transitions provide a reasonable picture of the processing requirements for the registration application.

Adding States To A View

The basic building block of the state transition model is the state entity. The relationships between states represent the transitions.

Set the Zoom Level:	1	From the **View** menu, select 66% zoom so that you can see all of the needed workspace.
Create a New Diagram:	2	From the **File** menu select **New Diagram**.
	3	Select the diagram type State Transition Diagram.
	4	Select Standard Workspace.
	5	Click OK.
Add States:	6	Click the first symbol button, the rectangle, on the control bar. This is the state object.
	7	Place the cursor in the middle of the diagram workspace and click the left mouse button. A state object is drawn.
	8	Label this state "Registered."

	9	Add the rest of the state objects as shown in Figure 9-1.
Save the Diagram:	10	Save the state model with the label "Registration States."

Adding Relationships To The State Model

The relationships in a state model define the transitions that occur to produce the various states. The transitions are events or triggers that cause the state to change from one value to another.

Build Relationships:	1	Select elbow line type in the control bar and begin the connections from the state of Never Registered to Registered. This process is similar to the one used in defining entity relationships.
	2	Label the transition "Vehicle is Purchased."
	3	Continue the relationship labeling until the model is complete, as shown in Figure 9-1.
Save:	4	Select Save from the File menu.

Note

☐ The state model is the dynamic view of the objects in the class model. The Nest process can be used to link the class objects to their dynamic state transition diagrams. To do this return to your class diagram and select the Registration class. Then choose Nest/Explode from the File menu.

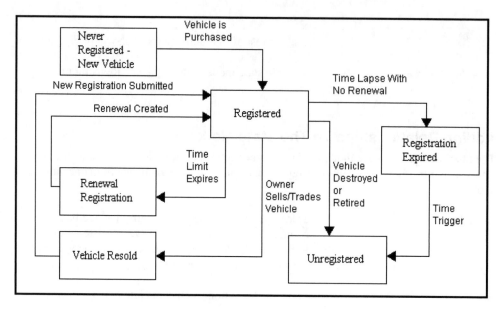

Figure 9-1 Completed State Transition Diagram

Lesson 10

Activity Diagramming

OVERVIEW

The activity diagram describes the sequencing of activities, with support for both conditional and parallel behavior. An activity diagram is a special form of a state diagram in which the states represent the performance of actions and the transitions are triggered by the completion of the actions. The activity diagram can be attached to a class or to the implementation of an operation or a use case. The purpose of an activity diagram is to focus on flows driven by internal processing (as opposed to external events). Usually activity diagrams are constructed in situations where all or most of the events represent the completion of internally-generated actions.

DEFINITIONS

The main components of an activity diagram include:

Activity (State)   An activity is a state of doing something. It could be a task such as receiving a payment, or the execution of a software routine, such as a method on a class. It is represented by a rectangle with rounded corners.

Decision   A decision is used when more than one activity can be performed next, based on a certain condition. There is a single incoming transition and several guarded outgoing transactions. The guards are mutually exclusive and so only one of the outgoing transactions is followed. A diamond denotes the decision start and end.

Merge   A merge marks the end of the conditional behavior started by a decision branch. The merge is also represented by a diamond (the same symbol that denotes the beginning of the conditional behavior).

Synchronization Bar   A synchronization bar is used to show parallel activities. It is represented by a black bar with one or more input transitions and one or more output transactions that are all taken in parallel. This means that the sequence of the output transactions is irrelevant. In order to show that all the parallel activities need to be completed before the following activities, use a second synchronization bar that has multiple incoming transactions and a single outgoing transaction. The outgoing transaction is taken only when all the incoming transactions are completed.

Start
The start object designates the starting point of the activity diagram and is represented by a filled circle.

End
The ending point of the activity diagram is represented by a filled circle inside a hollow circle.

Swimlane
A swimlane is a way of designating responsibility for each action state. An activity diagram may be divided visually into "swimlanes", each separated from neighboring swimlanes by vertical solid lines on both sides. Each action is assigned to one swimlane.

Transition
Represented by a solid line with a stick arrowhead, transitions may cross swim lanes. Transitions are implicitly triggered by the completion of the preceding them. The transitions may include guard conditions and actions. It is labeled by a transition string of the form 'Event [guard]/Action'. All components of the transition string are optional.

RELATIONSHIPS

The relationship structure in an activity diagram is directional arrows showing the order in which the activities occur. Parallel activities end at a synchronization bar, signifying that these activities must be completed before the succeeding activity may occur.

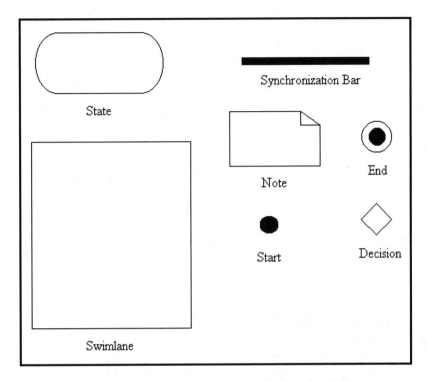

Figure 10-1 Activity Methodology Symbols

DEVELOPING YOUR ACTIVITY DIAGRAM

An activity diagram is a variety of activity states arranged in the sequence in which they must be performed. For our tutorial example, we look at the process of getting a driver's license.

Designating the Starting Point

For every activity diagram there has to be a designated starting point, represented on the diagram by a filled circle.

Set the Zoom Level:	1	From the **View** menu, select 66% zoom so that you can see all of the needed workspace.
Create a New Diagram:	2	From the **File** menu, select New Diagram.
	3	Select the diagram type Activity.

	4	Select Standard Workspace.
	5	Click OK.
Add Start:	6	Click the fourth symbol button, the filled circle, on the control bar. This is the start object.
	7	Place the cursor in the top center of the workspace, and click the left mouse button. The starting point is drawn on the diagram.
Save the Diagram:	8	Save the activity diagram with the label "Driver's License Activity Diagram".

Adding A Synchronization Bar

A synchronization bar is used to depict activities performed in parallel. The bar signals the start and end of parallel activities. In our example, the receiving clerk can receive the application form and proof of insurance simultaneously. It is not important in which order the items are received. However, the next activity, validating the applicant, can only be performed after both the application and the proof of insurance are received.

Add Synchronization Bar:	1	Click the third symbol button, the bar, on the control bar. This is the synchronization bar that denotes forks and joins.
	2	Place the cursor under the start circle and click the left mouse button. A synchronization bar is drawn.
	3	Add the other bar as shown in the Figure 10-2.
Save the Diagram:	4	Save the activity diagram.

Adding Activities

Activities are the basic building blocks of the activity diagram. By determining what activities need to be performed and arranging them in the order in which they are performed, with support for conditional and parallel behavior, the activity diagram is complete. Activities are represented by rectangles with rounded corners, with the activity text described inside the rectangle.

Add Activities:	1	Click the first symbol button, the rectangle, on the control bar. This is the activity (state) object.
	2	Place the cursor under the start circle and click the left mouse button to add an activity object to the diagram. Label this activity "Receive Road Test Form/Learner's Permit".
	3	Add the rest of the activities as shown in the Figure 10-2.
Save the Diagram:	4	Save the activity diagram.

Adding Decisions To A View

In a process, some activities may occur only if a certain condition is met; otherwise, certain other activities are carried out. The decision diamond marks the beginning and end of conditional behavior. In our example, the testing procedure continues only if an applicant is deemed valid. Otherwise, the applicant is informed why his/her application was deemed invalid; and the driver's license application process ends.

Add Decision:	1	Click the second symbol button, the diamond, on the control bar. This is the decision object.
	2	Place the cursor under the activity "Validate Applicant" and click the left mouse button. A decision symbol is drawn.

	3	Add the other decision objects as shown in Figure 10-2.
Save the Diagram:	4	Save the activity diagram.

Adding Stopping To A View

The stopping point for a process is denoted with a filled circle inside a hollow circle.

Add Stop:	1	Click the fifth symbol button, the filled circle inside a hollow circle, on the control bar. This is the stop symbol.
	2	Place the cursor at the bottom of the diagram, as shown in Figure 10-2, and click the left mouse button. A stop symbol is drawn.
Save the Diagram:	3	Save the activity diagram

Adding Transitions To A View

Transition lines are arrows that communicate the order in which the activities are to be performed. They can be labeled or left unlabeled.

Turn Off Auto Label Lines:	1	Select the Options menu and uncheck Auto Label Lines.
Add Transition:	2	Click the horizontal arrow symbol button on the control bar, labeled event. This is the transition symbol.
	3	Place your cursor on the start object. Left-click the mouse and hold down the button as you drag the cursor down to the first synchronization bar.
	4	Add the rest of the transitions as shown in the Figure 10-2.
Save the Diagram:	5	Save the activity diagram.

Adding Labels to Transition Lines

Select the Transition to be Labeled:	1	Click on the transition leading to the activity "Perform Driving Test" so that the line is highlighted.
Add Transition:	2	Right-click the mouse and choose **Change Item**.
	3	Type 'valid' in the Event Name field and click OK.
	4	Add the rest of the labels as shown in the Figure 10-2.
Save the Diagram:	5	Save the activity diagram.

Adding Swimlanes To A View

Swimlanes depict responsibility. You can use swimlanes to depict which people or departments are responsible for which activities. In programming, this translates to assigning a class to each activity. In our example, we can identify two DMV departments that would be responsible for the activities in our diagram. The applicant testing department would perform the actual tests and evaluate the test results. The DMV administration staff would perform the other duties such as accepting applications, validating applicants, issuing licenses to qualified applicants, etc.

Add Swimlane:	1	Click the sixth symbol button, the rectangle, on the control bar. This is the swimlane object.
	2	Place the cursor above the start object and click the left mouse button. A swimlane symbol is drawn. Label the swimlane "DMV Administration".
	3	Click the control bar arrow to activate the select mode.

4   Select the swimlane you just drew and expand its size by a clicking and dragging at its ends. Make sure the activities that are DMV Administration's responsibility fall in this swimlane as shown in Figure 10-2.

5   Add the other swimlane as shown in the Figure10-2.

Save the Diagram: 6   Save the activity diagram.

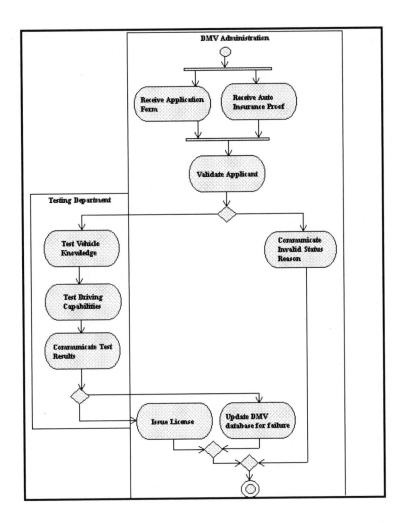

Figure 10-2 Activity Diagram

Lesson 11

Use Case Diagramming

OVERVIEW

A use case diagram is a representation of a set of activities that are performed to satisfy user goals. It is based on the premise that a user interacts with a business system to obtain benefits and satisfaction.

A use case diagram defines a set of transactions and the flow of events that occur from the time the user first starts using the system until the user's goals are satisfied. The use case diagram includes 'actors' representing the typical kinds of users that will interact with the system. The actors then communicate with 'use cases', representing the activities that are needed to satisfy the user goals.

The use case diagram focuses on 'what' a business process must do as opposed to 'how' a business process is implemented.

DEFINITIONS

A use case diagram includes the following components:

System Boundary	A system boundary is a rectangular box representing the business processes supported by an information system.
Use Case	A use case is an elliptical shape representing an activity included in an information system.
Actor	An actor is a stick person shape representing a role or a set of roles that a user plays.

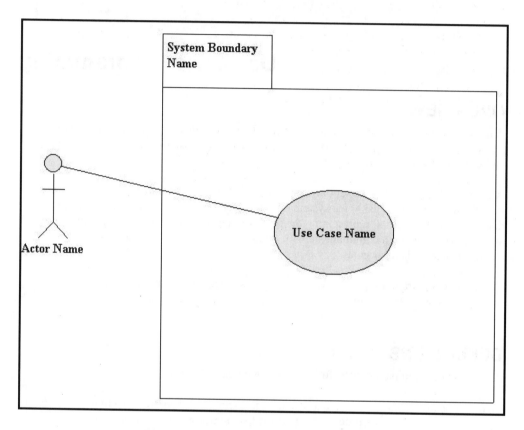

Figure 11- 1   Basic Use Case Components

The following general rules apply to the use case components:
* A use case symbol is positioned inside the system boundary.
* A use case diagram may include one or more use cases.
* An actor is positioned outside the system boundary.
* A use case diagram may include one or more actors.
* An actor communicates with one or more use cases.

RELATIONSHIPS

A relationship is represented as by a line from one object to another. The following relationships may be shown in a use case diagram:

- **Communicates**. The communicates relationship is represented by a solid line with no arrow, and is drawn between an actor and a use case.
- **Includes.** The includes relationship signifies that a use case contains behavior that is common to more than one use case. Thus the common use case is 'included' in the other use cases. The includes relationship is represented with a dashed line with an arrow. An includes relationship may exist between use cases, but not between actors. The arrow points to the common or shared use case. The stereotype is <<include>>.
- **Extends.** The extends relationship signifies that one use case possesses behavior that enables the other (extended) use case to handle an exception, or a variation from the usual. The extends relationship is represented with a dashed line with an arrow to the basic use case. The extends relationship may only exist between use cases (not between actors). When specifying an extends relationship, you may also specify one or more extension points. An extension point represents additional information that needs to be gathered in order to complete the transaction. The stereotype is <<extend>>.
- **Generalize.** The generalize relationship signifies that one thing is more usual or typical than the other thing. A generalize relationship may exist between two use cases, as well as between two actors. It is represented with a dashed line with an arrow. The arrow points to the use case (or actor) that generalize the other use case (or actor).

Examples of Relationships

The following is a discussion of the relationships presented in Figure 11-2.

- *Actor Communicates with Use Case*
  An example is an actor 'communicates' with a use case. This is the most common relationship found on use case diagrams.
- *Use Case 'Authorize Transaction' included in Use Case*
  The use case 'Deposit Cash' and 'Pay Bill' include the common use case 'Authorize Transaction'.
- *Actor 'Regular Customer' Generalizes Actor 'VIP Customer'*
  An example is an actor having a set of roles that 'generalize' another actor's roles. For example, a 'regular customer' is a generalization of a 'VIP Customer'.
- *Use Case 'Arrange Financing' Extends Use Case 'Sell Automobile'*
  The extended use case provides additional steps concerning the setup of the loan. The basic use case 'Sell Automobile' involves a cash sale.

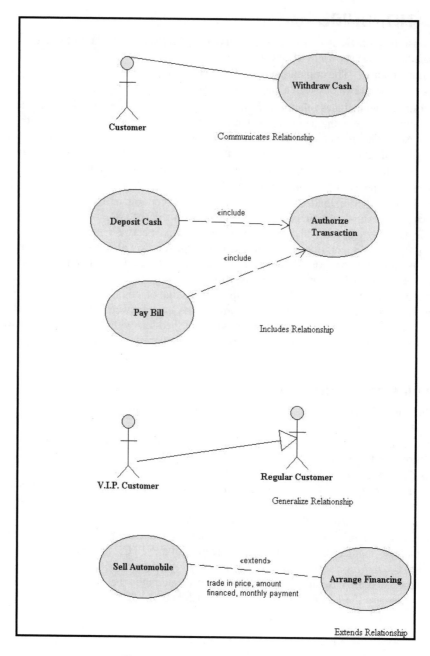

Figure 11-2 Use Case Relationships

DESCRIBING USE CASE ACTIVITIES

Visible Analyst provides the following basic attributes for describing a use case activity:
- **Name.** The name of the use case that appears on the diagram.
- **Description.** A brief description of the use case object.
- **Alias.** An alternate name for the use case. Up to ten aliases are permitted.
- **Scenario.** A complete description of the business scenario, up to 64K characters.
- **Notes.** Optional comments concerning the use case, up to 64K characters.

DEVELOPING YOUR USE CASE DIAGRAM

The business analyst creates one or more use case diagrams to fully explore the following questions:

Who will be the users of a business system?
Classify the kinds of users by defining an actor for each distinct role played by the users.

What goals does the system satisfy?
Consider the benefit or added value that the actor is seeking

What use cases are needed?
Consider the flow of events that will occur when a typical user who comes prepared with complete and accurate information and any prerequisites such as having enough cash or credentials. Make sure the use cases will satisfy the base case scenario. Then consider what activities are needed to handle the exceptions.

Ultimately, after exploring the above questions, you have one or more use case diagrams to create using Visible Analyst. Use the following procedures to create a use case diagram.

BUSINESS SCENARIO

The following is a business scenario that will be rendered using use cases.

An applicant visits a Department of Motor Vehicle's driver testing facilty, and provides the registrar with a personal details including name, address, and telephone number, as well as proof of automobile insurance and a learner's permit. The registrar schedules a driver road test and written examination with a certified driver examiner. After passing the theoretical and practical tests the applicant is issued a drivers licence.

There are two actors in this scenario: the registrar and the driver examiner.

- The registrar interacts with the system by registering applicants, by setting up appointments for driver tests, and by issuing drivers licences to successful applicants.
- The driver examiners interact with the system by scheduling their availability, and by conducting driver tests.

The objective is to create a use case diagram that includes the following use cases:
- Register Applicant
- Schedule Driver Test
- Conduct Driver Tests
- Issue Licence

Adding System Boundaries, Actors, and Use Cases

The following procedure enables the analyst to create a use case diagram and add system boundaries, actors and use cases.

Set the Zoom Level:	1	From the View menu, select 66% zoom so you can see all the needed workspace.
Create a New Diagram:	2	From the File menu select New Diagram.
	3	Select the diagram type Use Case Diagram.
	4	Select Standard Workspace
	5	Click OK.
Add System Boundary:	6	Click on the third symbol button, the rectangle, on the control bar. This is a system boundary.
	7	Label this system boundary "Driver Registration System".
	8	Select the system boundary to highlight the system boundary, and its sizing handles. Then adjust the size and position of the system boundary so there is enough room to the left of the boundary to place actors, and enough room inside the boundary to place use cases.
Add Actors:	9	Click on the first symbol button, the actor, on the control bar. Place the symbol on the diagram.
	10	Label this actor "Registrar".

	11	Add the rest of the actors as shown in Figure 11-3.
Add Use Cases:	12	Click on the third symbol button, the use case, on the control bar. Place the symbol on the diagram.
	13	Label the Use Case "Register Applicant".
	14	Add the rest of the use cases as shown in Figure 11-3.
Save the Diagram:	15	Save the use case diagram with the label Introductory Use Case.

Adding Relationships

The following procedure enables the analyst to add relationships to a use case diagram.

Adding a Communicates Relationship between an Actor and Use Case:	1	Select the first relationship button, the solid line **Communicates**. Begin the line on the actor "registrar" and end the line on the use case "Register Applicant". If you wish, you can label the line; or click Cancel to exit the label relationship dialog box.
Adding an Includes Relationship between Use Cases:	2	Select the third relationship button, the dotted arrow **Includes**. Begin the line on the use case "Register Applicant" and end the line on the use case "Collect Payment".
	3	Add the rest of the relationships as shown in Figure 11-3.
Save the Diagram:	4	Save the use case diagram.

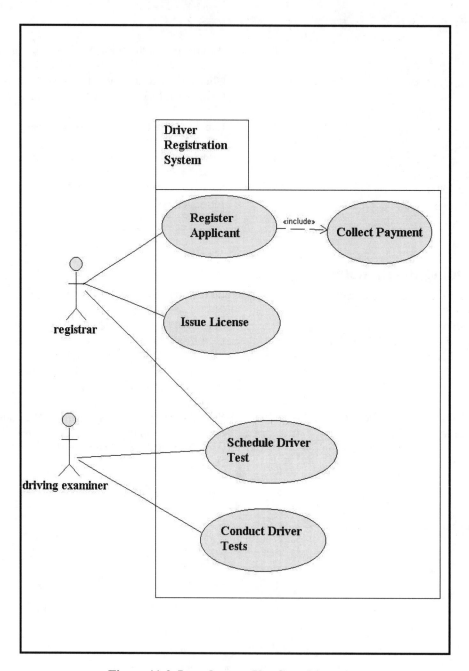

Figure 11-3 Introductory Use Case Diagram

Lesson 12

Sequence Diagramming

OVERVIEW

A sequence diagram is a type of interaction diagram. Interaction diagrams describe how groups of objects interact and collaborate in performing a behavior. There are two types of interaction diagrams that basically model the same information: sequence diagrams and collaboration diagrams. In a sequence diagram, the interaction is modeled in time sequence. Generally, an interaction diagram captures the behavior of a single use case. The sequence diagram shows several objects participating in the interaction and the messages that are passed among these objects. The diagram shows the objects by their "lifelines" and the messages that they exchange arranged in time sequence. It does not show the associations among the objects. The associations can be obtained from the complementary collaboration diagram.

A sequence diagram has two dimensions: the vertical dimension represents time and the horizontal dimension represents different objects. Normally time proceeds down the page. (The dimensions may be reversed if desired.) Usually only time sequences are important; but in real-time applications, the time axis could be an actual metric. There is no significance to the horizontal ordering of the objects. Often call arrows are arranged to proceed in one direction across the page; but this is not always possible, and the ordering does not convey information.

DEFINITIONS

The components of the sequence diagramming process include:

Object
: An object is defined as an instance of a class. It is drawn as a rectangle with the name of the object and class name inside the rectangle.

Class
: A class is a group of objects with the same data structure (attributes) and behavior (operations). A class is an abstraction that describes properties that are important to an application.

Lifeline
: The lifeline represents an object's life and existence during the time period of the interaction. A dashed vertical line is the symbol of a lifeline. An object symbol is drawn at the top of the lifeline.

Activation	An activation shows the time period during which an object is performing an action. It represents both the duration of the action in time and the control relationship between the activation and its callers. An activation is shown as a tall thin rectangle whose top is aligned with its initiation time and whose bottom is aligned with its completion time. Activation symbols are drawn on the top of an object's lifeline.
Message	A message is a communication from one object to another, usually communicating an order to perform an action. A message is represented by a horizontal solid arrow from the lifeline of one object to the lifeline of another object. The time order in which these messages occur is shown top to bottom on the page. Each message can be labeled with a message name, conditions, return arguments, etc.
Self Call	This is a message that an object sends to itself. It is represented by a message arrow originating at the object lifeline and looping around to end at the same lifeline.
Object Deletion	Objects that are deleted by a message or self-destruct during the time period of the interaction have a large X drawn at the bottom of their lifeline.
Return	A return is a message that is not a new message, but rather a return message from an object to which a new message was previously sent. It is labeled with a dashed line rather than a full line.
Condition	Some messages are sent only when a certain condition is true. In this case, you can label the message with the controlling condition.
Asynchronous Message	An asynchronous message is one that does not stop the caller object from continuing processing.

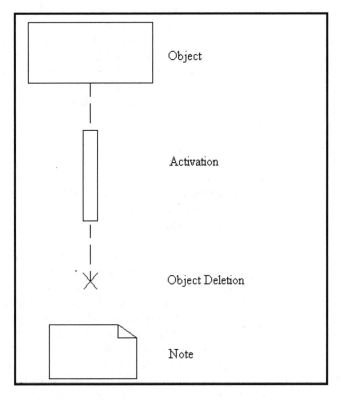

Figure 12-1 Sequence Diagram Symbols

DEVELOPING YOUR SEQUENCE DIAGRAM

The sequence diagram primarily is composed of a group of objects and the messages that are passed between them.

Adding Objects

Objects are the basic building blocks of the sequence diagram. The objects are usually placed horizontally across the page in no particular order, while the vertical axis denotes time sequence. Objects used on the sequence diagram may already exist in the repository, or they may be new objects created during the time period of the interaction.

Each object will have a dashed vertical line under it, representing its lifetime. If the object is created or destroyed during the period of time shown on the diagram, its lifeline starts or stops at the appropriate point. Otherwise, it goes from the top to the bottom of the diagram.

Set the Zoom Level:	1	From the **View** menu, select 66% zoom so that you can see all of the needed workspace.
Create a New Diagram:	2	From the **File** menu, select **New Diagram**.
	3	Select the diagram type Sequence.
	4	Select Standard Workspace.
	5	Click OK.
Add Object:	6	Click the first symbol button, the rectangle, on the control bar. This is the object symbol.
	7	Place the cursor in the top left of the workspace and left-click the mouse. The object is drawn and you are prompted for an object name and class name. Leave the object name field blank. Type "Application Entry Window" as the class name. Click OK.
	8	You are prompted to create a new class if it doesn't already exist. Click the Yes button.
	9	Add the rest of the objects as shown in the Figure 12-2.
Save the Diagram:	10	Save the sequence diagram with the label "DMV Sequence Diagram".

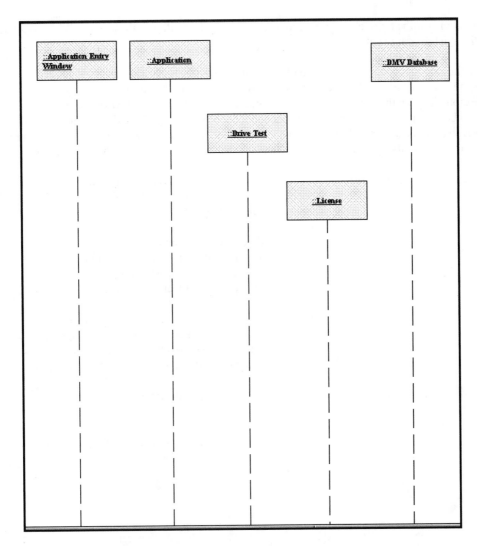

Figure 12-2 Sequence Diagram with Objects

Adding Activation Symbols

An activation represents the time period during which an object is performing an action. It represents both the duration of the action in time and the control relationship between the activation and its callers. An activation is shown as a tall thin rectangle whose top is aligned with its initiation time and whose bottom is aligned with its completion time. The incoming message may indicate the action. In procedural flow of control, the top of the activation symbol is at the tip of an incoming message (the one that initiates the action) and the base of the symbol is at the end of a return message.

In the case of a recursive call to an object with an existing activation, the second activation symbol is drawn slightly to the right of the first one so that they appear to "stack up" visually. Before drawing the second activation symbol, lengthen the size of the original activation symbol by grabbing the symbol handles when the object is highlighted. After drawing the second activation symbol on top of the first symbol, increase the width of the second symbol so that it visually "stacks up" over the first symbol.

Add Activation Symbol:	1	Click the second symbol button, the narrow vertical bar, on the control bar. This is the activation symbol.
	2	Place the cursor on the "Application Entry Window" object's lifeline, and click the left mouse button. An activation symbol is drawn on top of the object's lifeline.
	3	Add the other activation bars as shown in the Figure 12-3. You can size the length of the activation symbols by clicking on the rectangle and dragging the edges.
Save the Diagram:	4	Save the sequence diagram.

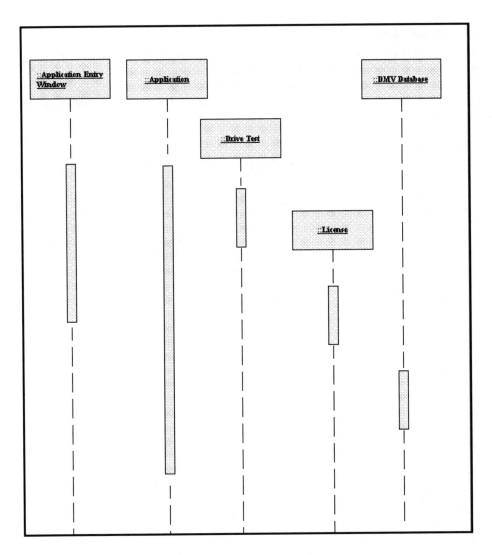

Figure 12-3 Sequence Diagram with Activation Symbols Added

Adding Object Deletion

Objects can be deleted during an interaction during the time represented on a sequence diagram. Objects that are deleted by a message or that self-destruct during the time period of the interaction have a large X drawn at the bottom of their lifeline. In our example, the object Application is created when a new application is received and is deleted after the application has been processed.

Add Object Deletion:	1	Click the third symbol button, the X, on the control bar. This is the object deletion symbol.
	2	Place the cursor under the "Application" object lifeline and click the left mouse button. An object deletion symbol is drawn. Add the other object deletion symbols as shown in Figure 12-4.
Save the Diagram:	3	Save the sequence diagram.

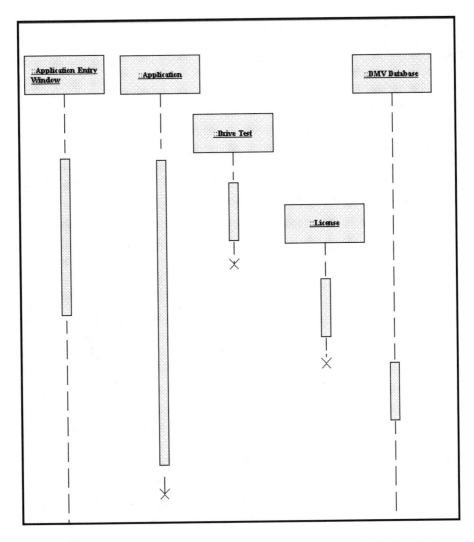

Figure 12-4 Sequence Diagram with Object Deletion Symbols Added

Adding Procedure Calls to the Diagram

Messages that are procedure calls can be passed from one object to another. It is basically a command for the receiving object to perform a certain action. When adding any message, there are certain pieces of information you are required to enter:

• **Name.** Name of the message.

- **Type.** A message can be of three types: procedure call, flat flow of control, or asynchronous stimulus.
- **Occurs Many Times.** This is a flag that indicates whether a message is sent many times to multiple receiver objects.
- **Guard Condition**. If the message is to be sent only if a condition is met, this field will contain that condition.

In our example, the object Application Entry Window submits an application to the object DMV Validation when a new application is accepted. This is an example of an unconditional procedure call. The Application object sends a message to the object License to create a new license. However, this message is sent only if the applicant passes the driving test. This is an example of a conditional procedure call.

Add Procedure Call:	1	Click the first arrow button, the bold full arrow on the control bar. This is the procedure call arrow.
	2	Place the cursor on the activation bar under the "Application Entry Window" object and click the left mouse button. Holding the left mouse button down, drag the cursor to the activation bar under the ""Application" object and release the left mouse button. The Label Message dialog box appears.
	3	The Label Message dialog box appears. Click New Method and type "New" for the name of the method. Click OK to return to the Label Message window. Click OK again to exit this window.
Add Procedure Call with Condition:	4	Place the cursor on the activation bar under the "Application" object and click the left mouse button. Holding the left mouse button down, drag the cursor to the activation bar under the "DMV Database" object and release the left mouse button.
	5	The Label Message dialog box appears. Click New Method and type "Update Success" as the method name. Click OK to return to the Label Message dialog box. Type "passed" in the guard condition field and click OK.

| | 6 | Add the rest of the procedure calls as shown in Figure 12-5. |
| *Save the Diagram:* | 7 | Save the sequence diagram. |

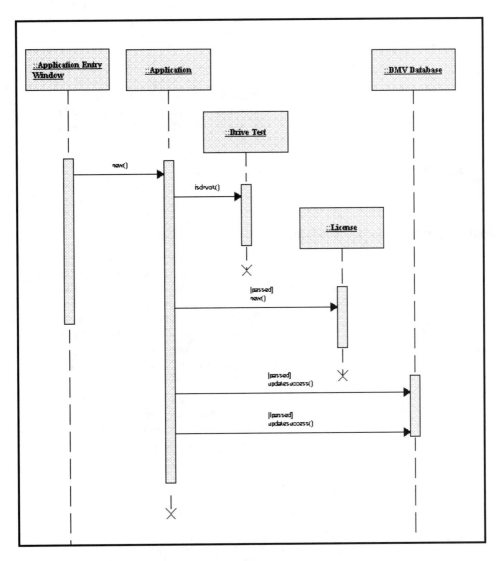

Figure 12-5 Sequence Diagram with Procedure Calls Added

Adding Return to the Diagram

An object can send a message in response to a message sent to it earlier. In our example, the application object returns the message sent to it by the application entry window object.

Add Return:	1	Click the fourth arrow button, the dashed arrow, on the control bar. This is the return symbol.
	2	Place the cursor on the activation bar under the "Drive Test" object and click the left mouse button. Drag the cursor to the activation bar under the "Application" and release the mouse button. A return arrow is drawn
Save the Diagram:	3	Save the sequence diagram.

Adding Text Notes to the Diagram

Add Note:	1	Click the rightmost button on the toolbar, an uppercase T. This is the Add Text button.
	2	Place the cursor under the procedure call isdrvok() and click the left mouse button. The Add Text window appears. Type "passed = isdrvok()" and click OK. The note is added to the diagram.
Save the Diagram:	3	Save the sequence diagram.

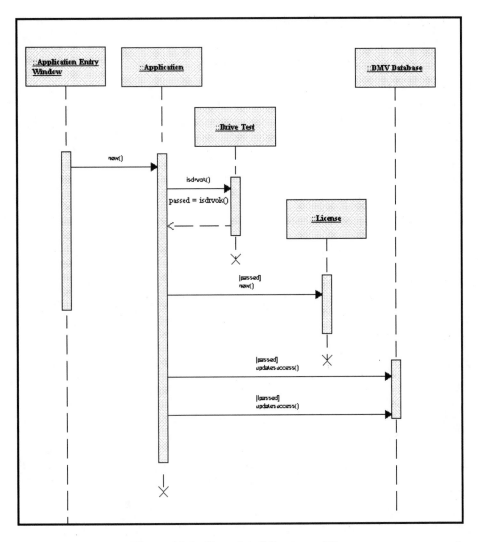

Figure 12-6   Completed Sequence Diagram

Lesson 13

Collaboration Diagramming

OVERVIEW

UML includes specifications for two forms of interaction diagrams: sequence diagrams and collaboration diagrams. Both diagrams present the objects participating in a business scenario and show the messages sent and received.

The sequence diagram uses 'lifelines,' parallel bars drawn below the objects, so that the sequence of messages sent and received can be understood by looking at the diagram from top to bottom. On the other hand, in a collaboration diagram the objects are arranged so that the basic relationships are highlighted; and sequence numbers are used to order the messages sent and received.

A collaboration diagram consists of a set of objects that together carry out a scenario, the links between the objects, and details concerning the messages sent and received. A collaboration diagram can be drawn at the class level or at the instance level.
- At the class level, it shows the associations or relationships between the different classes.
- At the instance level, it shows the links or messages that are passed between the instances.

DEFINITIONS

The important diagram constructs in collaboration diagrams include:

Object	An object appears in as a plain rectangle with an underlined title. It represents an entity with a well-defined boundary and identity that encapsulates state and behavior. A collaboration diagram may be populated with objects representing different classes, as well as objects representing specific instances in a class.
Note	A note appears as a rectangle with the top right corner folded over. A note is used to record descriptive text that appears on the diagram.

Object Link	An object link appears as a solid line connecting two objects and represents the fact that there is a relationship between the two objects. Visible Analyst automatically adds a message (as part of the task) when an object link is drawn between two objects.
Procedure Call	A procedure call is a message between two objects, appearing as a filled solid arrow. The target object (at the arrowhead end) must complete its task before the calling process can continue.
Flat Flow of Control	Flat flow of control is a message between two objects, appearing as a stick arrowhead and signifying the passing of control from the originating object to the target object.
Asynchronous Stimulus	Asynchronous stimulus is a message between two objects, appearing as a half-stick arrowhead, and used instead of a stick arrowhead to show an asynchronous communication between two objects in a procedural sequence.
Return	A return is a message between two objects, appearing as a dashed arrow with a stick arrowhead, and represents a return from a procedure call.
Self-Delegation	Self-delegation is a message from an object to itself, appearing as a recursive arrow.
Note Link	A note link appears as a dotted line connecting an object with a note.

DEVELOPING YOUR COLLABORATION DIAGRAM

Describing Scenarios using a Collaboration Diagram

The business analyst creates a collaboration diagram to explore the following questions:
- What objects are included in the scenario?
- What messages are sent and received?
- What is the sequence of the messages?

The objects that are included in a scenario are typically part of the enterprise model. For example, an object introduced to the repository using the class diagram can certainly be reused in a collaboration diagram. See Lesson 8, The Class Diagrams.

Object Instances Versus Object Classes

The objects appearing in a collaboration diagram may represent object instances or object classes. The way in which an object is identified determines if the object is an instance or a class. When the name is specified, it means this object represents a particular object instance. For example 'John Smith:: Applicant' represents the fact that 'John Smith' is a member of the 'Applicant' class. If no object name is specified, the object represents the class.

Note the object class must always be specified. The object identifier is separated into two parts using a double colon (::); the first part specifies the name, the second part the class.

Object Methods

The messages sent to and from an object must 'fit' the object, or correspond with its methods. Only methods from the derivation tree of the target (the one receiving the message) object's class can be used. All available methods are displayed in the drop-down list. If you want to create a new method, click the New Method button.

If the method has arguments, you can specify values for the arguments by clicking the Values button. By default the name and type for the method are displayed. If you want to change the argument list of the method, click the Change Arguments button.

Note

☐   The degree to which you can change method or message attributes depends on your rights to the target object's class and the interaction diagram settings.

Object Links

A Label Message dialog box appears when an object link is drawn between two objects. You must then supply details concerning the messages. If you are not ready to define these details (or wish to define them a later), you can delete the message icons, and retain the object link as a solid line.

Messages

Messages are added to the collaboration diagram to describe the way in which the objects will work together.

The following information is maintained for each message:
*   **To and From.** The name of the target object and source object. This can be switched by clicking the Reverse button.
*   **Type.** The type of message, either asynchronous stimulus, flat flow of control, or procedure call.
*   **Occurs Multiple Times.** Indicates the message will be called more than once. If this option is selected, an asterisk will appear next to the message name on the diagram.

- **Guard Condition.** Specify the guard condition that controls the firing of the message. This is a free-form text field. A guard condition is a logical expression that evaluates to TRUE or FALSE, and must be satisfied before the message can be sent.
- **Sequence Number.** Indicates the order of messages. This can be either a single numeric value such as 1, 2, or 3, or a decimal such has 1.2, or 1.1.4. This option is only available on collaboration diagrams, since sequence diagrams by their very nature indicate message ordering.

DEPARTMENT OF MOTOR VEHICLES SCENARIO

The collaboration diagram example is based on the following scenario:
- The registrar logs onto the system and selects the driver registration window.
- By selecting the option New Applicant, an Applicant object appears. Details concerning the applicant's name, address, and phone number are recorded.
- The registrar verifies that the applicant possesses an insurance certificate, and if yes, records the coverage limits. The registrar also verifies that the applicant has a learner's permit. Once these checks are made the applicant is considered 'Valid' and is ready for the road test.
- If the applicant passes the road test, a driver's license is issued.

A completed collaboration diagram is shown in Figure 13-1.

Adding Objects to a View

The basic building block of the collaboration diagram is the 'object'. The following steps are taken to establish a new collaboration diagram and create the objects.

Set the Zoom Level:	1	From the View menu, select 66% zoom so you can see all of the needed workspace.
Create a New Diagram:	2	From the File menu select New Diagram.
	3	Select the diagram type Collaboration Diagram.
	4	Select Standard Workspace and Portrait Orientation.
	5	Click OK.
Add Objects:	6	Click on the first symbol button, the rectangle, on the control bar. This represents an object.
	7	Place the cursor inside the diagram workspace and click the left mouse button.

	8	Label the object, leaving the name field blank, and the class field "Applicant".
	9	Add the rest of the objects as shown in Figure 13-1.
Save the Diagram:	10	Save the Collaboration Diagram, and give it the name 'Driver Registration'.

Adding Relationships to a Collaboration Model

The relationships in a collaboration diagram appear as object links. Messages to and from the objects are added to the object links.

This procedure was written with Auto Label Lines turned on; thus message details must be added when an object link is drawn.

Add Object Links:	1	Select the object link from the control bar and make a connection from 'Driver Registration Window' to 'Applicant'.
Add Message to the Object Link:	2	Select the method that is associated with the target object; or if no method exists, add a method. Add the method "new".
	3	Select the message type 'Flat Flow of Control'.
	4	Leave the guard condition blank.
	5	Enter the sequence number '1.1'.
	6	Continue adding messages until the model is complete, as shown in Figure 13-1.
Save:	7	Select Save from the File menu.

Note
- You can turn the display of messages, arguments, argument types, and guard conditions on or off by selecting Messages from the View menu.

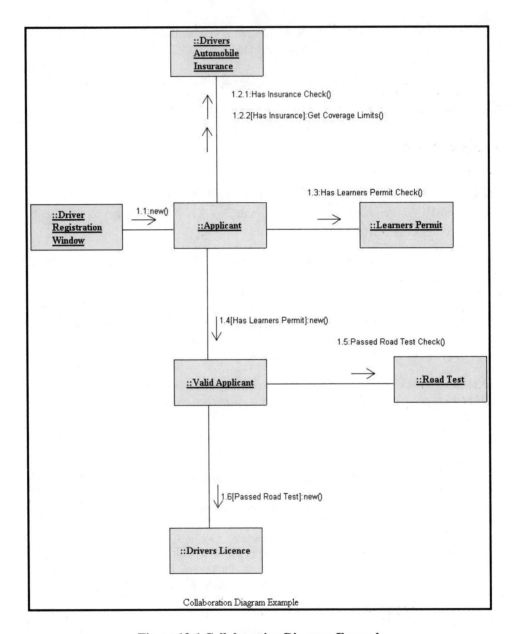

Collaboration Diagram Example

Figure 13-1 Collaboration Diagram Example

Lesson 14

Working with the Repository Functions

OVERVIEW

This unit helps familiarize you with the operation of the Visible Analyst repository and shows you the power of an online, interactive database for systems analysis, design and data modeling. The TEST project used in the previous lessons is used as the basis for your exercises.

The repository is a powerful tool for creating and managing the narrative portions of a system's specification. A project repository is used to provide an entry location for all project documentation. Each graphical entry on your diagrams has an automatically created corresponding entry in the project repository, as do any items entered into a Composition or Alias field.

You have the ability to thoroughly define all of your graphical entries in the repository or to simply enter notes about them in the Notes field. As an integrated part of Visible Analyst, the repository operates in parallel with the diagramming functions to accomplish data decomposition logically. It contains powerful data management, text editing, import/export, and report facilities. By using it, meaning can be ascribed to diagrams and an asset of ever-increasing value can be created. After defining items, changing entries and entering notes, you can generate reports from this information in many different forms.

When you finish defining your data and processing, the repository also allows you to put it into an ASCII file and export it. The ASCII file can then be sorted to move data specifications to your database and process specifications to your text editor for writing code. (The Shell Code Generation utility can also be used for this purpose.)

Note

□ Users of the Educational and Demonstration versions of Visible Analyst cannot add items directly into the repository. First add the object to the diagram, then edit it into the repository.

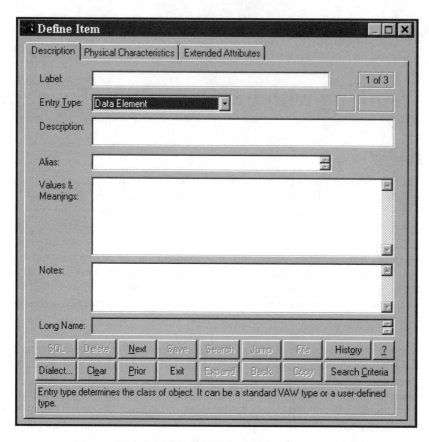

Figure 14-1 Blank Repository Dialog Box, Page One

REPOSITORY BASICS

Repository Control Buttons

The repository control buttons (see Figure 14-2) are always displayed at the bottom of the repository dialog box. Each of the button functions is accessed by clicking on the button, or, as is customary in Windows, by using its keyboard shortcut by holding down the ALT key and pressing the underlined letter to execute the button function. Only the functions available to you at a given time are active; the others are grayed. The button functions are:

Figure 14-2 Repository Dialog Box Control Buttons

SQL
This button opens the Generated SQL for View dialog box. This dialog box displays the SQL generated for the current view object based on the view table and column specifications selected when creating the view, as well as the current SQL dialect. This button is active only when the entry type is View.

Dialect
This activates the RDBMS SQL Dialect dialog box. From there, you can change the current SQL dialect.

Delete
This deletes the current repository entry from the database. An entry can only be deleted when it has no location references, meaning that it does not appear on a diagram nor in the composition of another repository item.

Clear
This clears the display of an entry and displays a blank repository dialog box. This allows you to Search for an existing entry or add a new entry. If you have made changes, you are prompted to save them before clearing. Your current location in the repository remains unchanged.

Next
This displays the next sequential repository entry that meets the repository search criteria (see below).

Prior
This displays the previous sequential repository entry that meets the repository search criteria.

Save
This saves all changes made to an entry.

Exit
This or the ESC key exits from the repository.

Search
This initiates a search for a particular entry in the repository. The procedure is explained in the section on Search Capabilities.

Expand
Contract
This allows you to expand or contract the display size of some fields. The fields that normally display four lines can expand to display 15.

Jump This allows you to jump immediately to another entry that is referred to in the current one. This feature is described in the section on Navigation Capabilities.

Back This button provides a means of jumping to the previous repository entry. You can then continue to move backwards displaying previous repository entries.

File This allows you to insert text from a DOS file at the cursor position or to copy highlighted text to a DOS file. It is explained in further detail in the Visible Analyst *Operation Manual* and in the online help system.

Copy This button provides a means of copying the current object.

History This provides a means of jumping back to a previously displayed repository object. A list is kept of every object definition that has been displayed. If you choose this button, the History dialog box appears and you can jump between entries by double-clicking on an entry. The maximum is 500 objects.

Help(?) This displays context sensitive help about the repository. You can also press F1 to activate the help system.

Search Criteria This allows you to specify how the repository is to be searched. It is explained in the section on Search Capabilities.

Other buttons that may be displayed on the Define dialog box are:

Primary Key If the current object being examined is an entity type, the primary key button is displayed to the left of the Composition/Attributes field.

Attributes Details This button provides a means of populating the composition of a repository entry with components and physical information. This button is displayed to the left of the Composition/Attributes field.

  When the Entry Type is a Class, or when the Classic User Interface is turned off, the Add button displayed beneath the Attributes Details button is active. You can use this button to add details. When you begin typing in the field next to the Add button, the button is enabled. Click the Add button to add the attributes to the Attributes field.

Editing Keys

Because the Edit menu is not accessible from the repository, you can use the right-click menu that is available when an object (text) is highlighted and you click the right mouse button. Using the right-click menu, you can Cut, Copy, Paste, or Delete the selected object.

Field Types

The data repository of a Visible Analyst project is displayed using Define dialog box variations corresponding to different diagram objects. You see and work with some of these variations during the course of this lesson. The basic dialog box, shown in Figure 14-1, is for data elements, aliases, miscellaneous objects and external entities or source/sinks. Other objects, such as data stores, processes, functions, entities, relationships, modules, data flows information clusters, etc., have variations in individual fields and tabs of the Repository dialog box to accommodate the specific needs of those items. Some of these differences are seen later in the lesson.

Label Field

This is the name of the repository item. The names of items drawn on diagrams are automatically entered here.

Entry Type Field

This tells Visible Analyst what kind of object the item is: process, data flow, entity, etc. The entry type can be entered manually, or you can select the type from the scroll box accessed by clicking the down arrow at the end of the entry type field.

Note
    You can edit the Entry Type and Label fields of data elements and data structures that do not appear on diagrams. The entry type for a data element cannot be changed if physical information for that element has been entered.

Description Field

The Description field is a two-line field that provides a convenient place to enter a somewhat more extensive descriptive title of the object than the Label field allows. The contents of this field are used for the Comment on Column (data elements) and Comment on Table (entities) when SQL DDL is generated if the selected SQL dialect supports this syntax.

Alias Field

The Alias field contains 10 lines of 128 characters each. It allows for the entry of alternative labels to the one used as the object label. This is most commonly used for indicating the cryptic abbreviations that are sometimes used in the actual coding of a software program, as opposed to the plain English names that are desirable for reference. The Alias field is an intelligent field. Data names entered into it establish new repository entries for these aliases.

Attributes Field

The purpose of the Attributes field is to accumulate the collection of data elements that you wish to define as constituting a data flow, entity, data store, etc. The Attributes field is an intelligent field. Data names entered into it establish new data element repository entries or update existing ones. These new data elements can then be used for further definition. Data flows, data structures and couples can also appear in some Attributes fields.

When you click the Attributes Details button, the Add Attributes dialog box appears. Using this dialog box, you can define up to 12 components and some of their properties. As you enter items, the dialog box automatically scrolls as necessary to allow you to enter more items until you reach 12. When you complete the entries, click OK to add them to the Attributes field. If you need to add more than 12 components, click the Attributes Details button again; and a new dialog box opens so that you can add more.

Use the Add button at the bottom of the Attributes field to add components one at a time. When you begin typing in the field next to it, the Add button becomes active. Complete your entry, and then click Add to enter the component in the Attributes field.

Values & Meanings Field

The Values & Meanings field allows an unlimited number of lines. The maximum number of characters that can be contained in the field is 64K. This field allows the entry of specific information about the value(s) the item can take.

Discriminator Values & Meanings Field

If the current object is a data element that is used as a discriminator, this field contains a list of values to identify the subtype entities. For each subtype, a value can be entered that will uniquely identify it. By default, these values are numbers starting with 0 for the supertype. To change the value, click the value until an edit control appears, make your changes, then press ENTER.

Notes Field

The Notes field is also a field that allows you to enter any pertinent information about the object. The maximum number of characters that can be contained in the field is 64K.

Location Field

This field displays two types of usage information. The field can contain the diagram name (and, for DFDs, the diagram number) of every diagram where the item appears. The field can also tell you if the item appears in the Composition field of another item. This second kind of location entry has the entry type of the parent item, followed by an arrow and the name of the parent item.

Other Pages and Fields

Other pages of the Define dialog box contain additional information. For example, pages 2 and 3 of the basic repository form provide location and relationship information and specifications for PowerBuilder/VISION extended attributes. These two pages are similar for most entry types. For some entry types, additional pages can be displayed:

- When the entry type is an entity, the next five pages contain keys, foreign keys, triggers, check constraints, and physical information.
- For views, the next five pages provide table, column, join, clause, and option information.
- When the entry type is a relationship, there are additional pages that contain foreign key and cardinality information.
- When the entry type is a tablespace, an additional page contains property information.

A full list and complete descriptions of pages and fields can be found in the *Operation Manual* and in the online help.

Object Repository

The Visible Analyst repository provides several additional forms and data input components for supporting the object-oriented concepts. The object repository components are detailed below.

Attributes

The Attributes field replaces the Values & Meanings field whenever the Repository dialog box displays a class. The field contains a list of the data members for the class showing the local data element and type. To add, change, or remove local data elements, click the Attributes Details button or select Add/Change from the Repository Object menu. For each attribute, the following information can be defined:

- **Name**. The name of the attribute. Each attribute of a class has a separate entry in the repository with a type of local data element. This is an optional field. The search button can be used to find other local data elements in the repository.
- **Type**. The attribute type can be a class, data element, or data structure. If the type does not exist in the repository, a new class is created. The location field of the attribute type contains a reference to the current class. This is a mandatory field. The Search button can be used to display a list of valid types. If the attribute type is a data element or elemental

class, its physical characteristics are displayed. Entries added to the Type field are saved as data elements for an entity or data flow, and class/subtype element when the object is a class.

- **Limit**. The number of occurrences of the attribute. If this field is blank, the attribute occurs once.

- **Reference**. A qualifier to indicate the access method for an attribute. *Value* indicates the object defined in the *Type* field is used; *Address* indicates a pointer to the object is to be used; and *Reference* indicates a reference to the object is to be used. The default is Value.

- **Visibility.** *Public* members have global visibility. *Private* members are only accessible to member functions and friends. *Protected* members are accessible to derived classes and friends. *Implementation* members are only accessible to the class itself. The default is Private.

- **Qualification**. *Constant* indicates a member's value cannot be changed. *Volatile* indicates the member can be modified by something other than the program, either the operating system or hardware. *Static* indicates there is only one instance of the member regardless of the number of times a class is instantiated. The default is None.

- **Physical Characteristics**. If the attribute type is elemental, the physical characteristics can be set.

For every item entered into the Type field, Visible Analyst creates a repository entry (if one with the same name does not already exist) and updates that entry's location field. If an item is removed, this field is updated to reflect this. These repository entries are generally created as classes unless a data element already exists with the same name or the physical characteristics are defined

As you enter items, the dialog box automatically scrolls as necessary to allow you to enter more items until you have finished. Insert is used to insert a new attribute into the list at the current position, while Delete removes the current attribute (the current position is indicated by ➤➤). When you have completed the entries, click OK to add them to the Attributes field.

Item names entered into this field may contain up to 128 characters each and may consist of any upper or lower case letters, numbers, spaces, periods, underscore characters and hyphens; but the first character must always be a letter.

Attached Entities/Classes

The attached entities/classes for the currently displayed relationship are listed in this field. When an inheritance relationship is displayed, the characteristics of that relationship can be changed (see changing Inheritance Characteristics later in this chapter). Otherwise, the information cannot be edited from within the repository; and all changes must be made on a diagram. The field lists the two entities or classes attached to this relationship. Below the second entity name is listed the reverse of the current relationship. If either direction of the relationship has not been named, the name of the relationship in the reverse direction is displayed as "reverse of (opposite relationship name)." This field allows you to jump to the repository entries for any of these entities or relationships, as described above.

Relations

For an entity or class, the Relations field displays the relationship name followed by the name of the entity or class on the other end of this relationship for each relationship attached to this entry. These sets are ordered alphabetically by the opposite entry name. When an inheritance relationship is displayed, the characteristics of that relationship can be changed (see Changing Inheritance Characteristics later in this chapter); otherwise, the information cannot be edited from within the repository; and all changes must be made on a diagram.

This field allows you to jump to the repository entries for any of these entities, classes, or relationships by positioning the cursor on the line containing an entity, class, or relationship name and clicking the Jump button.

Long Name

When a repository entry, either a local data element or a module, belongs to a class, the full name of the entry includes the class name. The Long Name field displays this name and, in the case of modules, includes the argument list (the argument list is required to differentiate overloaded member functions). If you want to change the argument list for a class method, click the right mouse button on the Long Name field and select Change (see the Methods section later in this chapter for details). If you want to change the class to which the method belongs, select Class from the Repository Object menu. To display the class definition, click the Jump button.

Class Characteristics

Concurrency, displayed on the Methods/Friends tab, is a class property that distinguishes an active object from inactive object. An *active* object may represent a separate thread of control. A *sequential* object is a passive object whose semantics are guaranteed only in the presence of a single thread of control. A *guarded* object is a passive object whose semantics are guaranteed in the presence of multiple threads of control.

A persistent class exists beyond the lifetime of an executable program. This means it must be stored on a non-transitory storage device. If the subtype of a class is set to either entity (associative or attributive) and the class is used on an entity relationship diagram, this field cannot be changed.

An abstract (or virtual) class cannot be instantiated because it contains pure virtual methods. If pure virtual methods exist for a class, Abstract is checked. If you attempt to uncheck this field, all pure virtual methods are reset to virtual. If you attempt to check it and virtual methods exist, they are converted to pure virtual methods.

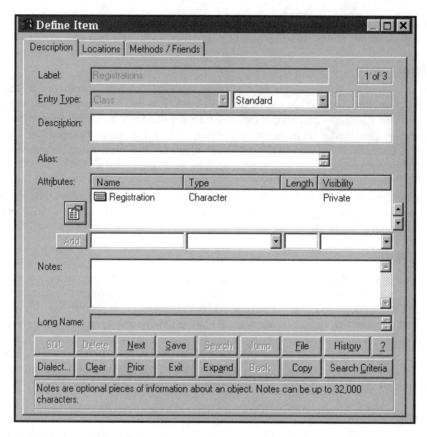

Figure 14-3 Class Attributes

Methods

Methods (or Member Functions) are the operations that are defined for accessing a class. The Methods field contains a list of the functions for a class showing the name, return value, argument list, and flags to indicate its visibility. To add, change, or remove methods, click on the Methods field and click the Attributes Details button or select Add/Change from the Repository Object menu. To add a new method for a class, click the New button and type the name of method you wish to add. To search for methods that have already been defined in the repository, click the Search button. The list contains all modules that have previously been defined in the repository. If the module already belongs to a class, the class name is displayed. Note that when you select a module that already exists, the complete definition for that module is used including return value and argument list. Click OK to add the method name to the list of methods for the current class. For each method, the following information can be defined:

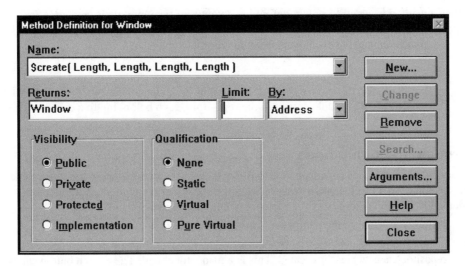

Figure 14-4 Class Methods

- **Returns**. The return type can be a class or data element. If the type does not exist in the repository, a new class is created. The Location field of the attribute type contains a reference to the method. This is an optional field. Click the Search button to display a list of valid types.

- **Limit**. The number or size of the parameter. If this field is blank, it occurs once.

- **By.** A qualifier to indicate how the return value is passed. *Value* indicates a copy of the parameter is passed; *Address* indicates a pointer to the object is to be used; and *Reference* indicates a reference to an object is to be used.

- **Visibility**. *Public* methods have global visibility. *Private* methods are only accessible to other member functions within the same class and friends. *Protected* methods are accessible to derived classes and friends. *Implementation* methods are only accessible to the class itself. The default is Public.

- **Qualification**. *Static* indicates a method can be used without a specific instance of an object (it can only be used with static attributes (data members)). A *Virtual* method is one that you expect to be redefined in a derived class. A *Pure Virtual* method has no definition and must be defined in a derived class. A class with any pure virtual functions is an abstract (or virtual) class. The default is None.

- **Arguments**. A list of parameters to be used by the method. This is an optional field. If a method appears more than once with the same name within a class, it must have a different argument list for each definition. This is known as function overloading. See the next section for defining arguments.

When a method is added to a class definition, an entry of type module is created in the repository. The long name includes the class name and the argument list. The argument list is needed to differentiate between overloaded functions.

Note

▢ Because the same name can be used for more than one method, there may be duplicate module entries in the repository, each belonging to a different class.

Arguments for Methods

When defining methods (member functions) for a class, the parameters to the function need to be specified. To add, change, or remove arguments, click the Arguments button on the Method Definition dialog box. For each argument, the following can be defined:

- **Name**. The name of the parameter. This is an optional field.

- **Type**. The parameter type can be a class or data element. If the type does not exist in the repository, a new class is created. This is a mandatory field. The Search button can be used to display a list of valid types. If the parameter type is a data element or elemental class, its physical characteristics are displayed.

- **Limit**. The number or size of the parameter. If this field is blank, it occurs once.

- **Pass By**. A qualifier to indicate the how the parameter is passed. *Value* indicates a copy of the parameter is passed; *Address* indicates a pointer to the object is to be used; and *Reference* indicates a reference to an object is to be used. The default is Value.

- **Qualification**. *Constant* indicates a parameter's value cannot be changed. *Volatile* indicates the parameter can be modified by something other than the program, either the operating system or hardware. The default is None.

- **Physical Characteristics**. If the parameter type is elemental, the physical characteristics can be set.

For every item entered into the Type field, Visible Analyst creates a repository entry (if one with the same name does not already exist). These repository entries are generally created as classes unless a data element already exists with the same name or the physical characteristics are defined.

As you enter items, the dialog box automatically scrolls as necessary to allow you to enter more items until you have finished. INSERT is used to insert a new parameter into the list at the current position, while the DELETE key removes the current parameter (the current position is indicated by ▶▶). When you have completed the entries, click OK to update the method name field. Item names entered into this field may contain up to 128 characters each and may consist of any upper or lower case letters, numbers, spaces, periods, underscore characters and hyphens; but the first character must always be a letter.

Friends

The Friends field displays a list of both friend classes and methods (or functions). A friend is allowed access to the private data members of a class. To add friends, click on the Friends field and click the Search button, select Add from the Repository Object menu, or double-click on the Friends field while pressing CTRL key. A list of classes and member functions is displayed in the Search list box. Locate each repository item you want to place in the Friends field and click the Search button; the item is added to the Select list box at the bottom. When you have found all of the entries you want, click the Select button and they are entered into the Friends field.

To remove a friend, highlight the desired item and press the DELETE key or select Cut or Delete from the Repository Object menu.

Navigation Capabilities

In this section, you change the displayed repository entry using Next, Prior, and Jump.

Note

⌂   The repository saves some internal settings for the duration of a Visible Analyst session. If these are set incorrectly, they may interfere with the smooth flow of this lesson. Therefore, we suggest that if you or another user worked in the repository during the current session, you should exit to Windows and restart Visible Analyst. In this way, you have a clean slate on which to run this lesson.

Open the Repository:	1	Access the repository using either **Define** from the **Repository** menu or CTRL+D. A blank Define dialog box is displayed.
Access an Entry:	2	Type "Person Information" in the Label field and press ENTER twice. (Pressing ENTER once brings up the Search dialog box. Pressing it a second time displays the entry found. If you press ENTER twice quickly, you get the same result without displaying the search box.) The repository entry for Person Information displays with all of the information that has been entered into the repository for this entry.
Move Around:	3	Click Next. The next entry in alphabetical order is displayed.
	4	Click Prior. Person Information is again displayed.

Jump to Other Entries:	5	Click the element Name in the Attributes field. (It may be necessary to scroll the contents of the field to bring Name into view.) Click Jump. (Click Yes if you are asked if you want to save Person Information.) The repository entry for the data element Name is displayed.
	6	Move to page two by clicking the Physical Information tab at the top of the dialog box. (The current page number is displayed in the upper right corner of the Define window.) This displays more information about the current entry, including the Location information that indicates where the current entry is used.
	7	Click the line in the Location field containing Person Information. This highlights the line.
	8	Click Jump. The entry for Person Information is once again displayed. The Locations tab (page 2) is currently displayed. An alternative to selecting Jump to switch to another repository entry is to double-click the entry name in the Location field or to click the Back button.
	9	Move to page one by clicking the Description tab.

Search Capabilities

Searching for entries in the repository is an easy procedure. It can also be a very useful feature because you can set the Search Criteria to display only certain entry types as you move from one repository entry to the next. To search for an entry in the repository:

Access an Entry:	1	Click Clear. This clears the dialog box but does not delete the entry.
	2	Type "Road Test" and press ENTER twice. The repository entry for Road Test is displayed with all of the information that has been entered into the repository for this entry. (This was done for you in the samples included with the TEST project.)
	3	Click Clear.

Search for the   4   Click the Search button to open the search box to select
Entry: from the repository. Type "r" and entries that begin with
"r" appear in the list box. If you now type an "o," you see
that the repository searches incrementally as you type,
getting closer to the entry you want.

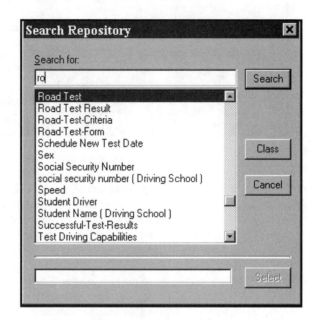

Figure 14-5 Repository Search Dialog Box

      5   Click Road Test and then click Search. The repository
entry for Road Test is displayed.

Setting the Search Criteria

Search criteria set the scope of the entries that are displayed as you search through the
repository.

Clear the Dialog Box: 1   Click Clear to clear the dialog box.

Set the Criteria: 2   Click Search Criteria. You see a dialog box
entitled Set Search Criteria, as shown in Figure 14-6.

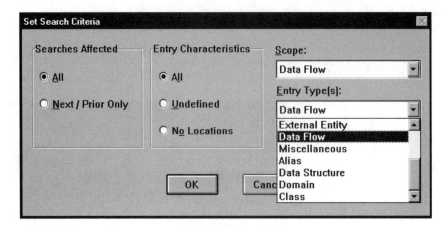

Figure 14-6 Setting Repository Search Criteria

3   In the box entitled Searches Affected, select All. This is the method used to limit the scope of the entries displayed when navigating the repository using Next and Prior, as well as the entries that are displayed when you select Search.

4   In the box labeled Entry Characteristics, select All. This tells Visible Analyst to search all items in the repository, rather than only those entries that are Undefined or entries that have No Locations. No Location entries are typically those that have been entered directly into the repository rather than added to the repository by being placed on a diagram.

5   Click the down arrow on the right side of the field marked Scope. This allows you to choose the diagram type to which you wish to limit your search. Select Data Flow.

6   Click the down arrow on the right side of the field marked Entry Type(s). This allows you to be very specific about the type of entry to which you wish to limit your search. You can choose individual types and some combination types.

7   Select Data Flow, and then click OK.

Try Out the Criteria:	8	At the blank Define dialog box, click Search. Because your search criteria limits searches to data flows, the list displays only the entries in the repository of the type data flow. Select Road-Test-Criteria and then click Search.
	9	Now click Next. The next entry displayed is the next *data flow* in alphabetical order, rather than simply the next *entry* in alphabetical order. If you click Next a few more times, you notice that only data flow entries are displayed.
	10	Click Search Criteria again and set Scope back to Entire Repository. Be sure that Entry Type(s) is set to All. Click OK.

Using Search to Add Items to a Field

The Search feature can also be used to add repository entries to a field without retyping them. This option is very useful for adding multiple data elements to an Attributes field. Instead of typing the name into the field, you can select it using the Search function.

Clear the Dialog Box:	1	Click Clear.
Find an Entry:	2	Type "V" in the Label field and click Search. Valid-Applicant should be the first entry on the list. Click on it and it appears in the Search For field. Click Search and the repository entry for Valid-Applicant appears.
Select Attributes:	3	Click on the Attributes field.
	4	Click the Search button. The available data elements are displayed. Double-click on Address, Birth Date, Name, and Social Security Number. All the selected elements are displayed at the bottom of the Search dialog box as shown in Figure 14-7.

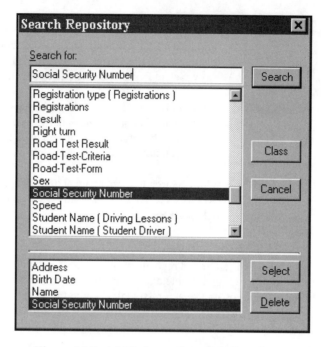

Figure 14-7 Add Information with Search

Add Attributes   5   Click Select. All the selected elements are added to the
and Save: Attributes field. Click Save and then click Exit.

ADVANCED REPOSITORY FEATURES

Adding Information to the Repository

In this unit, you add attribute information to an entity; the attributes consist of the data
elements that make up the entity. You also add the primary key information, so that you can
demonstrate Key Analysis and Key Synchronization to migrate foreign keys across
relationships automatically. All of the key information relates to the method for accessing
tables in a database. We assume that each entity corresponds to one table.

Open a Diagram: 1   Open the entity relationship diagram Driving School
                       View.

Display a Repository Entry:	2	Click the ↖ button on the control bar.
	3	With the *left* mouse button, double-click the entity Student Driver. Its repository entry is displayed.
Enter Attribute Data:	4	Place the text entry cursor in the field immediately to the right of the Add button under the Attributes field. Type "Student Name" and click Add. Add "Home Address" and "Age" in the same manner. Since the data elements you just added to the Attributes field are not already in the repository, entries for each are automatically added when you click Save.
Save the Entries:	5	Click Save to save the attributes you entered.
Enter Key Information:	6	Click the key button to display the Primary Key dialog box. Select Student Name to move it from the Columns in Table box to Columns in Key box. Click OK to return to the Define dialog box.

The key notation by Student Name indicates that Student Name is the primary key for this entity.

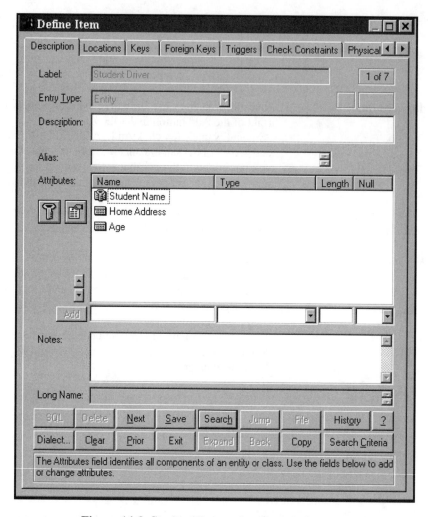

Figure 14-8 Student Driver Attribute Information

Clear the Dialog Box:	7	Click Clear. This clears the repository dialog box but does not delete the entry from the repository.
Access Another Entry:	8	Type "Driving School" in the Label field and press ENTER.

Add Composition:	9	Click the Attributes Details button and type "Driving School Number" and "Driving School Name," each on a separate line. Click OK.
Create Primary Key:	10	Click the Key button next to the Attributes field to display the Primary Key dialog box.
	11	Click Driving School Number in the Columns in Table box to move it to the Columns in Key box. Click OK to return to the Define dialog box.
Save:	12	Click Save to save your changes, then click Clear.
Access Another Entry:	13	Type "Driving Lessons" in the Label field and press ENTER.
Add Attributes:	14	Click the Attributes Details button, place the cursor in the Type field, and then click Search.
	15	Scroll the search box until Driving School Number appears. Click Driving School Number and then click Search to enter it on the Attributes dialog box. Move the cursor to Type field of the next line. Add Student Name in the same manner.
	16	Move the cursor to the Type field of the next line, and type "Lesson Number." Click the cursor in the Limit field to enable the Physical Characteristics pane at the bottom of the dialog box. Select Integer as the Data Type.
	17	Click OK to add the attributes to the Define dialog box.
Create Primary Key:	18	Click the Key button next to the Attributes field to display the Primary Key dialog box.
	19	Click Lesson Number in the Columns in Table box to move it to the Columns in Key box. Click OK to return to the Define dialog box.
Save and Exit:	20	Click Save and then click Exit.

Key Analysis and Key Synchronization

The Key Analysis and Key Synchronization functions, found on the Repository menu, can help you set up a consistent relational database key structure. There are three types of keys used in a data model: primary, foreign, and alternate keys. All keys are designated in the Attributes field of an entity in the project repository. A primary key is one or more attributes or data elements that uniquely identifies an entity. To designate a data element as a primary key, the yellow key notation is used in the Define dialog box. On the diagram, primary keys are displayed in the area immediately under the entity name when the primary key level is selected from the control bar or the View/Entity Display Options menu. A foreign key is a non-key attribute in one relation that appears as the primary key (or part of a compound primary key) in another relation. The gray key notation in the Attributes field of an entity designates a foreign key. The AK notation is shown when the entity on the diagram is displayed at the attribute view level.

Key Analysis verifies that the key structure for your data model is complete, checking that all key information is correctly identified for the data model. Key Synchronization analyzes the key structure and migrates data elements that you designate as keys, or parts of compound keys, across relationships to their associated entities, and creates the resulting foreign keys. Using associator element names in relationship repository entries makes this process work better. (Please check the Visible Analyst manual or online help system for an explanation of associator elements.)

Key Analysis and Key Synchronization both involve analyzing the primary key [PK] and foreign key [FK] designations in the TEST project repository. A primary key is an attribute or data element that uniquely identifies a record.

Run Key Analysis: 1   Select Key Analysis from the Repository menu. Visible Analyst scans the entire repository and indicates any errors it finds.

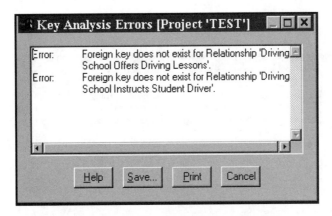

Figure 14-9 Key Analysis Error Messages

View the Errors: 2   Click the Maximize button in the upper right corner of the errors dialog box. Scroll through the messages. You see that there are error messages indicating missing foreign keys for the entities on the current diagram.

Note

▢   You can keep analysis error dialog boxes on the screen while you carry on various Visible Analyst activities. This is to make it easier for you to correct the errors found by **Analyze**. The same holds true for SQL Schema Generation, Shell Code Generation, etc.

3   Click Cancel.

4   Select **Key Synchronization** from the **Repository** menu. Visible Analyst first analyzes for key errors and then migrates the foreign keys across relationships.

5   Maximize the Key Synchronization Messages dialog box. Key Analysis messages appear first, followed by Key Synchronization messages. You should notice the Key Synchronization messages, indicating the foreign keys that have been migrated.

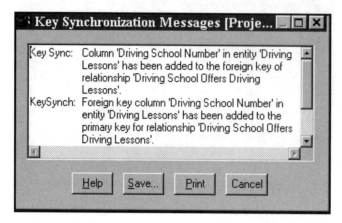

Figure 14-10 Key Synchronization Messages

6   Click Cancel.

Examine the   7   Double-click Student Driver. Notice the foreign key
Migrated Key: Driving School Number that has been added. This was
                           done by **Key Synchronization**. It saves you from
                           migrating all of the foreign keys manually.

                           Note also that **Analyze** added text describing the key. All
                           text following an asterisk is considered a comment and is
                           ignored by the repository. (When the object interface is
                           enabled, comments are not displayed.)

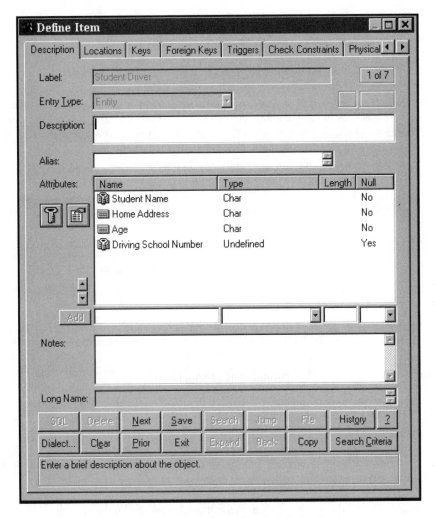

Figure 14-11 New Foreign Key Information

8   Click Exit.

9   Deselect Student Driver on the diagram.

View Objects

Visible Analyst Corporate Edition supports the concept of an SQL view, which can be thought of as a derived or virtual entity. A view is similar to an entity in that it has a composition, but the items that appear in the composition of a view must belong to other entities or be expressions based on data elements used by another entity.

An SQL view is made up of two major components: a list of column names and a select statement that is used to filter information from the tables in the view. The select statement can contain not only the primary select clause, but also any number of sub-selects and union selects. When view is selected as the entry type, view-specific Define dialog box pages are displayed. Using these pages, you can select tables, columns, join relationships, clauses, and other options for the view. An expression builder is available to help you create the expressions to be used in the filter, group by, having, start with, connect by, or join expression controls.

Detailed information about views can be found in the *Operation Manual* and in the online help system.

Note

☐ Views are not available in the Education Editions of Visible Analyst.

Generate Database Schema

The Corporate Edition of Visible Analyst generates SQL DDL (Structured Query Language – Data Definition Language) schema from the information contained in the repository. In the Corporate Edition, you can select from several different dialects of SQL, including a User Defined type, to allow the use of a dialect not currently supported by Visible Analyst. For more information on the custom feature, see the *Operation Manual* or the online help system. The statements that are supported include CREATE TABLE, CREATE INDEX, and COMMENT ON. More information is contained in the *Operation Manual* or in the online help system.

The Education Editions of Visible Analyst allow you to generate SQL for Microsoft Access and Oracle only. To generate SQL:

Choose Access Dialect:	1	Choose **SQL Dialect** from the **Options** menu, then choose **Access**. (Users of the Education Editions should skip this step.)
Generate SQL Schema:	2	Select **Generate Database Schema** from the **Repository** menu to generate the schema. When the dialog box appears, click OK. (Refer to the *Operation Manual* or online help system for details of the SQL Schema Generation dialog box.) If errors are found, they can be displayed, as well as the generated schema.
View the Schema:	3	Maximize the SQL generation dialog box.

4   Click the Schema button to display the generated schema.
See Figure 14-12. If Visible Analyst does not have the
information to generate the schema, a list of errors is
displayed; but no Select box is present. Click the Errors
button to view any errors. (If too many errors are
generated, the Schema button is not displayed.)

```
CREATE TABLE Department_of_Motor_Vehicles
(
    DMU_Number          INTEGER NOT NULL,
    Address             CHAR(30),
    Number_of_Evaluators  INTEGER,
    Number_of_Evaluators  INTEGER,
    Evaluator_Number    NUMBER,

    CONSTRAINT PKC_Department_of_Motor_Vehicles0000 PRIMARY KEY ( DMU_Numb
);

CREATE TABLE DMU_Evaluator
(
    Evaluator_Number         NUMBER NOT NULL,
    DMU_Number               INTEGER NOT NULL,
    Evaluator_Name           VARCHAR(40),
    Evaluator_Address        VARCHAR(60),
    Evaluator_Phone_Number   VARCHAR(12),

    CONSTRAINT PKC_DMU_Evaluator0001 PRIMARY KEY
        ( Evaluator_Number, DMU_Number ),

    CONSTRAINT FKC_employs0002 FOREIGN KEY ( DMU_Number ) REFERENCES
        Department_of_Motor_Vehicles
```

Figure 14-12 Generated SQL Schema

Shell Code Generation

The Corporate Edition can generate C and COBOL shell code. The code that is generated
encompasses the sequence of functions or paragraphs that make up a program, including
global definitions, descriptive comments, function call/PERFORM statements, and passed
parameters. Information entered in text fields in the repository entry for a program item or a
structure chart module produces comments that describe these items within the generated
code. Also, actual source code can be entered in the module description field of a module or
macro, and this code is placed in-line with the function calls or PERFORM statements that are
generated by invocations. Couples or ITRs used with invocation lines generate parameters for

C code. There is also an option to customize the code to be generated. (See the online help for other generation options supported by Visible Analyst, such as AS/400 DDS, Visual Basic, PowerBuilder, etc.)

XML Generation

Visible Analyst can generate XML DCD code based on the data models. This is similar to SQL schema generation. XML can be selected as the generation option when you select SQL Dialect from the Options menu. The procedure is similar to the SQL DDL generation. See the *Operation Manual* or the online help for more information.

Repository Reports

Now you practice generating a report on the data contained in the repository. This is a basic report containing a detailed listing of all entries contained in the repository. For detailed information about Reports and Report Queries (Custom Reports), see the *Operation Manual* or the online help system.

First set the font for the report you want to generate.

Set the Report Font:	1	From the **Options** menu select **Text Settings**.
	2	Under Text Type, select Report Body.
	3	Select a typeface and point size, and click OK.
Set the Report Criteria:	4	Select **Reports** from the **Repository** menu. The Repository Reports dialog box appears (see Figure 14-13).

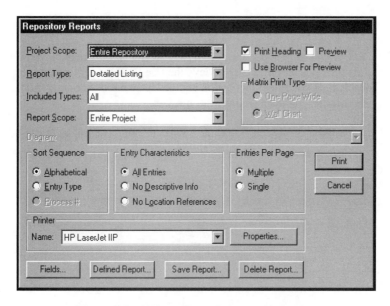

Figure 14-13 Repository Reports Dialog Box

5	Under Project Scope, select Entire Repository.
6	Under Report Type, select Detailed Listing.
7	Under Included Types, select All.
8	Under Report Scope, Entire Project is selected.
9	In the box labeled Sort Sequence, select Alphabetical. This determines the entry order in your report printout.
10	In the box labeled Entry Characteristics, select All Entries.
11	In the box entitled Entries Per Page, select Multiple Entries Per Page. You can select Single Entry Per Page to reorder the pages of your report once they have been printed.

Run the Report: 12   Click Print; the information is sent to the printer. Select Preview to view the report first.

Note

⬭ Reports can be generated in HTML format so that they may be viewed in a browser. When you select Preview, the Use Browser for Preview Option is enabled. If you select this option and you have a browser on your PC, the report is generated and displayed in your browser.

13   Click Cancel when printing is complete to exit the Repository Reports dialog box.

Lesson 15

Where To Go From Here

OVERVIEW

This concludes the Visible Analyst tutorial. To exit the program, select Exit from the File menu.

You have now completed exercises in many of the major elements of planning, structured analysis and design, data modeling and object modeling:

- Drawing diagrams to model a system.
- Using methodology rules to insure against inconsistencies.
- Adding written definition to the graphic model.
- Embellishing the model following the initial layout.
- Expanding the model through definition of repository elements.
- Generating reports.

All structured software and systems engineering involve these same basic operations.

REAL WORLD APPLICATION

The example project that you created was a simple one. The real power of CASE is in the application to systems too complex to keep in your head at one time, too large to be reviewed by inspection, too widespread to have only one person working on the whole job. These types of projects include nearly every system designed today. That power shows itself in four areas:

- The assurance of accuracy and completeness, that no elements are left dangling or unaccounted for.
- The prompting and reminders that error checks and repository output provide, to focus attention in the midst of a dauntingly complex assignment.
- The word processing-like ease with which changes and modifications can be accomplished, while ripple effects are flagged and accounted for.
- The convenience of thorough documentation that is produced concurrently with the design, not as a drudgery-filled after-effort.

The power of CASE further multiplies into substantial gains in productivity, communication and quality when applied to team effort. The Corporate Edition of Visible Analyst has significant capabilities for exporting and importing information, either through portable media or through participation in a local area network. This allows Visible Analyst to become an integral part of any development environment, sharing information and expanding the value of labor. Many groups thus can benefit from another group's hard work.

Finally, the application of the power of CASE productivity enhancement is not limited to software but can be applied toward analyzing and designing any system, such as:

Manufacturing	Medical Diagnostic Analysis
Planning	Command and Control Operations
Processing	Administrative Procedures
Legal/Judicial	Inventory Control
Audits	

Visible Analyst is designed to be a natural extension of the way you think, create, and analyze. Our goal is to "Put CASE Within Everybody's Reach" and to make CASE tools and the methodologies of structured analysis, design, data modeling and object modeling a natural, seamless, integrated part of your everyday work, rather than an arcane ritual to be occasionally endured by specialists. The integration and flexibility to use the components and elements that you deem necessary for your application provide you with a customizable tool set that can be adapted to support how you choose to work on the design and development of information systems.

WHAT TO DO NEXT?

There are still many things for you to do to become comfortable and committed to the use of a CASE tool. We suggest the following:

- Study and review the logic concepts introduced in the tutorial (consider reviewing the referenced materials).

- Review the tutorial steps and practice any areas that were unclear.

- Select a personal real-world project to do using Visible Analyst. Make it a modest-sized effort to give you some time to explore and experiment with the tool.

- Select the parts and components that you want to use in your software development practice.

- Practice, practice, practice. Make adjustments where needed.

- Make the tool a regular part of all of your projects.

- Define standards and procedures for library components.

- Build disciplines and skills with concepts and Visible Analyst.

- Use technical support as neededXdon't get stuck, don't become frustrated.

- Stop and evaluate what you have done, show others, review the work of othersXfind ways to improve the content and the processes.

- Practice reusability wherever possible.
- Stay up to date with the tool and the evolving methodologies.
- Build a library of materials for use in future projects.

CONCLUSION

We hope that these lessons have helped to make you feel comfortable with the planning, structured systems analysis and design, and data modeling tools, and their implementations in our product.

For more information or if you have any questions about CASE or structured analysis, please contact the Visible Systems technical support staff:

Telephone	(781) 778-0200
FAX	(781) 778-0208

Internet: http://www.visible.com
E-mail: support@visible.com

You can send your comments to:

Customer Comments
Visible Systems Corporation
201 Spring Street
Lexington, MA 02421

Index

D

V

W

X

Y

Z